The Religious Drama

Christian Classics Revived

The Publishers endeavor herein to make reaccessible to Researchers, Academics & Libraries worldwide Reproduced Editions of such rare and time-honored publications which continue to stand out for their cultural & historical importance, over the years. In this Series we'll focus on Christian Faith & Living vis-à-vis topics like Literature & Poetry, Indigenous Philosophizing, Ethical response towards Agriculture, Health & Healing, Science & Technology, Ecofeminist Theology, Sociological approach towards Human Rights, Law & Politics, Arts, History of Ideas, Ancient Civilizations, Cultural Contiguity, Religious Cosmologies & Mysticism, Footsteps of famous Theologians, World Peace & Harmony, Global Capitalism, Network Marketing, Cybertheology, Population & Demographics, Epigraphic Studies, Contextualized Education, and many others. We welcome your comments on our this effort and further suggestions for taking up any such scholarly titles, having gone in oblivion, befitting Classic Works of glorious and legendary writers on Christian Studies.

PASSION PLAY AT VALENCIENNES, 1547.

Reproduced from C. M. Gayley's *Plays of Our Forefathers*, by permission of Messrs. Duffield & Co.

Christian Classics Revived - 5

The Religious Drama

An Art of the Church

(Beginning to 17th Century)

By

Gordon Crosse

With Twenty-Six Illustrations

CWI

Christian World Imprints™

Christian World Imprints(TM)
Christian Publishing & Books from India
H-12 Bali Nagar, **New Delhi-110015**
info@christianworldimprints.com
www.ChristianWorldImprints.com
Phone: +91 11 25465925 Fax: +91 11 25173055

ISBN 13: 978-93-5148-007-5
ISBN 10: 93-5148-007-0

Originally published as a part of 'The Arts of the Church'

Printed at Chawla Offset Printers

EDITOR'S NOTE

THE little volumes in the ARTS OF THE CHURCH series are intended to provide information in an interesting as well as an accurate form about the various arts which have clustered round the public worship of GOD in the Church of CHRIST. Though few have the opportunity of knowing much about them, there are many who would like to possess the main outlines about those arts whose productions are so familiar to the Christian, and so dear. The authors will write for the average intelligent man who has not had the time to study all these matters for himself; and they will therefore avoid technicalities, while endeavouring at the same time to present the facts with a fidelity which will not, it is hoped, be unacceptable to the specialist.

TO

MY FATHER

PREFACE

THE purpose of this book is to supply a short sketch of the story of the drama as an art of the Christian Church from its beginnings to the present day. Portions of this story, notably those which bear on the development of the secular drama, have formed the subject of many learned works. But there does not seem to be any one book which covers the whole ground. Though it is not to be supposed that so small a volume as the present can fill so large a deficiency, it can at any rate attempt to outline the history of the Christian drama as a connected whole, and, in so doing, to vindicate its claim to the designation of a religious art.

A short bibliography has been added, which it is hoped may be of use to those who wish to study the subject more fully. In it will be found the full titles of those works of which, for the sake of space, only the authors' names are given in the footnotes.

I have to thank the Right Rev. Dr. Gore, Lord Bishop of Oxford, and Miss Cowan, of S. John's, Red Lion Square, for their kindness in furnishing me with descriptions of contemporary foreign plays which they have seen; the Rev. C. L. Marson for information about the Hambridge Nativity Play, of which he is director; and the Hon. and Rev. Canon J. G. Adderley and the Editor of this series for much kindly interest and assistance.

G. C.

CONTENTS

LIST OF ILLUSTRATIONS

The Arts of the Church

THE RELIGIOUS DRAMA

CHAPTER I

The Drama and the Early Church

THE right of the Drama to a place among the Arts of the Church will scarcely be questioned save by those who deny its claim to rank as an art at all. In all countries and at almost all ages of its history the Church of CHRIST has made use of the arts as aids to worship and as means of instruction. The arts of the poet, the musician, the architect, the painter, the sculptor, have served, in the common phrase, as the "handmaids of religion," in beautifying the Church and its worship, and assisting the teacher to penetrate and uplift the minds of his hearers. Each art has its special function. That of the drama, the representation of a story by means of dialogue and action, clearly renders it specially appropriate for the instruction and edification of the beholders. And, as this book will endeavour to show, it has so been employed by the Church. But the very qualities which make it, when properly used, specially effective as a power for good, also render it liable to abuse as an agent of evil. And this fact has at various times caused it to be altogether banned by Christians, who have concluded that it must be totally incapable of being turned to good uses. The same Puritan argument, as it may be called, has from time to time been applied to other arts, such as painting.

At the opening of the Christian era this attitude may be said to have been forced upon the Church; the theatre had fallen into unspeakable degradation.

The great tragic and comic dramatists were overshadowed in popular favour by sensuous exhibitions which inevitably contaminated the minds of the spectators. With such a stage the Church could make no terms. As far as possible Christians were forbidden to attend the theatre; and actors who were converted must give up their profession before Baptism.

After the conversion of Constantine (A.D. 312) this rigid attitude had to be somewhat modified. But the theatre retained its infamous character. There was never any question of Christianizing it. Consequently the Christian drama, when in due time it made its appearance, owed nothing to the Greek and Roman dramatists of antiquity, but derived an entirely independent origin from the services of the Church itself.

Such attempts as were made at Christian adaptation or imitation of the classical drama were mere literary exercises cast in dramatic form, such as the Χριστὸς

Πάσχων, a drama on the Passion formerly attributed to S. Gregory Nazianzen, but now proved to be an eleventh or twelfth century work. It professes to be written "after the manner of Euripides," from whom and from Aeschylus many of its lines are borrowed. Similar works appear to have been composed for scholastic use at a much earlier date.

But the most notable Christian dramas on the classical model are the six Latin comedies of Hrotsvitha (Hrotsuit), who flourished in the second half of the tenth century. She was a nun of the Benedictine Convent of Gandersheim in Saxony, and wrote poems and chronicles as well as the comedies. They are imitated from those of Terence with the declared object of substituting Christian for profane subjects, and piety for obscenity. Her style, as a rule, is dull and vapid, but though her plots are based in a general way on Christian martyrology, her treatment of them is apparently original, and, considering the time and circumstances, shows real genius. One of the most striking is that of *Abraham*. A hermit, hearing that his niece has fallen into evil courses, goes in disguise to seek her; in a vivid and realistic scene he poses as a would-be lover, and then, discovering himself, wins her to repentance. The same theme reappears in *Paphnutius*, where the hero reclaims a courtesan by a similar device. The other plays are chiefly concerned with martyrdoms, virginity, and miraculous conversions. In *Dulcitius* a scene of broad farce is introduced. It is named after a Roman official to whose custody the Emperor Diocletian hands over three Christian maidens who refuse to apostasize. Dulcitius imprisons them in his scullery, and on visiting them is stricken with madness, and embraces and kisses the pots and pans by mistake for the maidens. His face and clothes are blackened, and he is taken by his soldiers for a demon.

There is quieter but genuine humour in *Sapientia*, where a Christian matron, being asked her daughters' ages by the persecutor, bewilders him by wrapping them up in abstruse mathematical calculations.

Such episodes as the battle in *Gallicanus*, or that in which minutely described tortures are applied to the maidens in *Sapientia*, make it more than improbable that these plays were ever meant to be acted. They may have been read or recited by a number of speakers representing the various characters. It is possible that they are the sole survivors of a school of monastic drama, though there is no evidence for the existence of such a school in England at any rate. It is certain, however, that dialogues, whether of independent growth or ultimately based on the ancient drama, were a favourite device for conveying instruction. They formed a religious counterpart to the "disputations," called in English *strifs* or *estrifs*, in French *débats*, which formed an important part of the stock-in-trade of the secular minstrel. A typical subject was provided by Ps. lxxxv. 10. Two twelfth-century versions of this theme exist, one of which is ascribed to Stephen Langton, afterwards Archbishop of Canterbury. Mercy and Peace plead on behalf of sinful humanity, whose punishment is demanded by Truth and Righteousness. Eventually the Divine Plan of Redemption is unfolded and the disputing Virtues are reconciled.

Such dialogues foreshadow the later morals in which the actors are personified qualities. In this connection it is worth while to notice that the characters in Hrotsvitha's *Sapientia* include not only that matron herself but her three daughters Faith, Hope, and Charity.

Another religious *estrif* is the thirteenth century *Harrowing of Hell*, a dialogue probably intended to be recited by a single minstrel, who would impersonate, in turn, the Expositor who introduces the theme, our LORD, Satan, the Doorkeeper of Hell, and the spirits who are delivered from his charge. This subject occurs in the miracle cycles, and one at least, the *Ludus Coventriae*, borrows directly from the poem. Such dialogues and didactic poems, as well as plays like Hrotsvitha's, if any such existed, may have contributed to the development of the religious drama. But all these early experiments in dramatic form, though entitled for this reason as well as for their intrinsic interest to a place in its history, yet lack the great essential of drama, the unfolding of a story in action. These academic compositions may have influenced it at a later stage, but for the true beginnings of Christian drama we must look to another quarter, and one entirely independent of all extraneous sources.

CHAPTER II

The Liturgical Drama

WHEN the Church, in abhorrence of the foul stage of Imperial Rome, set its face against the theatre altogether, it reckoned without two very powerful forces: first the mimetic instinct, the passion for pretending to be some one else, which is deeply implanted in the human breast; and secondly the essentially dramatic nature of the Christian story and of Christian worship. We have already seen how Christian teachers instinctively adopted the dialogue form for conveying instruction; realizing that a conversation between personified virtues and vices, or between scriptural characters, arrests the attention, and carries conviction far more forcibly than a mere exhortation or narrative. And, further, no story is in itself more dramatic than that of the Gospel. The appearance on earth of the Divine Champion of humanity, His conflict with the powers of evil, culminating in the climax of apparent failure and defeat on Good Friday, followed by the dramatic reversal of fortune in the triumph of Easter Day—here was a subject made to the hand of the Christian dramatist. And the form which it was to take was determined by the dramatic nature of Christian worship.

Its chief service, the Mass, was both an actual reproduction of the words and actions of the Last Supper and a symbolic representation of the Atoning Sacrifice. Other instances of the use of drama were the Palm Sunday procession representing the entry into Jerusalem (which was already performed in the fourth century along the actual route of our LORD's entry); the recitation of the

Holy Week Gospels by different readers impersonating the chief actors in the story; and the washing of feet on Maundy Thursday. An interesting example, not taken from the Gospels, is to be found in the ceremonial for the dedication of a church. The bishop and his procession approach the closed doors from without, but one of the clergy is placed within. Three blows with a staff are given on the doors, and the anthem is raised, "Lift up your heads, O ye gates," etc. The question, "Who is the King of Glory?" is asked from within, and when it is answered the doors are opened, and as the procession sweeps through, he who was concealed within slips out, *quasi fugiens*, to join the train. It is a dramatic expulsion of the spirit of evil.[1]

These are examples of the readiness with which Christian worship lent itself to dramatic uses. But the actual germ

[1] Abbreviated from Chambers, ii. 4.

of the liturgical drama has been found in antiphonal singing, a practice which is thought to owe something of its origin both to Hebrew methods of psalmody and to the semi-choruses of the Greek theatre. Versicle and response soon found a place in Christian services, a line or verse sung by half the choir, or by a single chanter, being answered by the other half or by the full choir.

From early times also melodies without words, sung merely to vowel sounds, were included in the service. In the eighth and ninth centuries these *iubila*, as they were called, were greatly extended, and words were written to be sung to them. These interpolations, known as tropes, were introduced into the Mass at various points, and were based on passages of Scripture appropriate to the season. Schools of trope-writers arose in the ninth century, the best known being those of Northern France, and of the Benedictine monastery of S. Gall, near

Constance. The fact that some tropes took dialogue form may be attributed to the practice of antiphonal singing already mentioned. The most famous is the *Quem queritis*, which led up to the Introit at the Easter Mass. In its earliest form it runs:

> "Quem queritis in Sepulchro, Christicolae?"
> "Iesum Nazarenum crucifixum, o caelicolae."
> "Non est hic: surrexit sicut praedixerat.
> Ite, nuntiate quia surrexit de sepulchro."

> "Whom seek ye in the sepulchre, ye followers of CHRIST?"
> "JESUS of Nazareth, Who was crucified, O heavenly ones."
> "He is not here: He is risen, as He said;
> Go, tell the news that He is risen from the sepulchre."

This is obviously based on the Gospel account of the holy women at the tomb. At first it may have been sung in unison by the whole choir, but the words naturally lend themselves to antiphonal singing, half the choir taking the part of the angels and half that of the women. In the tenth century, if not earlier, a further and most important step in dramatic development was taken. The dialogue was now not merely sung by the two halves of the choir without action, but by individuals actually impersonating the speakers.

Our earliest definite evidence for this innovation is to be found in the *Regularis Concordia*, a body of rules for the Benedictine monasteries of England, apparently drawn up by S. Aethelwold, Bishop of Winchester, about 970. The following extract[1] from it may be taken as describing the ceremonial in use at Winchester at that date :

"While the third lesson is being chanted let four brethren vest themselves. Let one of these, vested in an alb . . . approach the sepulchre without attracting attention, and sit there quietly with a palm in his

[1] Abbreviated from the translation in Chambers, ii. 14.

hand. While the third respond is chanted, let the remaining three follow . . . bearing in their hands thuribles with incense, and stepping delicately as those who seek something [let them] approach the sepulchre. . . . When therefore he who sits there beholds the three approach him like folk lost and seeking something, let him begin in a dulcet voice of medium pitch to sing *Quem quaeritis.* And when he has sung it to the end let the three reply in unison *Ihesu Nazarenum.* So he, *Non est hic* [etc.]. At the word of this bidding let those three turn to the choir and say *Alleluia! resurrexit Dominus!* This said, let the one, still sitting there, and as if recalling them, say the anthem, *Venite et videte locum.* And saying this, let him rise, and lift the veil, and show them the place bare of the cross, but only the cloths laid there in which the cross was wrapped. And when they have seen this, let them . . . take the cloth, and hold it up in the face of the clergy, and as if to demonstrate that the LORD has risen . . . let them sing the anthem, *Surrexit Dominus*. . . . When the anthem is done let the prior, sharing in their gladness, . . . begin the hymn, *Te Deum Laudamus*. And this begun, all the bells chime out together."

It will be noticed that the trope has now assumed a more elaborate form; has been transferred from its original place in the Mass to the office of Mattins; and, more important still, has acquired additional significance as a sequel to another piece of symbolism. The ceremony of the Adoration of the Cross on Good Friday, itself as old as the fourth century, was in the tenth followed by its burial or *depositio* in a sepulchre. The *Concordia* directs: "Let the likeness of a sepulchre be made in a vacant part of the altar. . . . Let the deacons who previously carried the cross come and wrap it in a cloth in the place where it was adored. Then let them carry it back . . . until they come to the place of the monument, and there having laid down the cross as if it were the buried body of our LORD JESUS CHRIST, let them say an anthem. And here let the holy cross be guarded with all reverence until the night of the LORD's Resurrection." On Easter morning it was to be removed and set up "in a fitting place."

Here we have a symbolical drama. The place of the Adoration stands for Calvary. The cross representing the Sacred Body is taken thence to the sepulchre, a watch is set,[1] and on Easter morning the cross is raised up again. In the *Concordia* we find all this symbolism linked on to the *Quem queritis* by the use of the empty sepulchre and linen cloth as accessories to that dialogue; and so the process of linking-up representations of various portions of the Bible story begins.

[1] "It is an example of the irrepressible mediaeval tendency to *mimesis* that [the watchers] were sometimes accoutred like the knights of Pilate."—Chambers, ii. 23.

How it might be carried on will appear from a comparison of the various extant forms of the *Quem queritis*. In that last quoted the women announced the Resurrection to the choir. This naturally recalls their telling the news to the Apostles, and it was an easy step further to allow two chanters to stand out from the rest as representing S. Peter and S. John. A dialogue with the women beginning

> "Dic nobis Maria,
> Quid vidisti in via?"

was then followed by the incident of the two Apostles running to the sepulchre.

These episodes constitute the sequence *Victimae paschali* which followed on the *Quem queritis* when it had taken its place in the Mass. The following translation is given in the *English Hymnal* (No. 130). The women return from the sepulchre singing,

> "Christians, to the Paschal Victim
> Offer your thankful praises!
> A Lamb the sheep redeemeth:
> CHRIST, Who only is sinless,

Reconcileth sinners to the FATHER ;
Death and life have contended
In that combat stupendous :
The Prince of Life, Who died, reigns immortal."

They are met by the two Apostles who question them :

"Speak, Mary, declaring
What thou sawest wayfaring."

The *First Mary* replies :

"The Tomb of CHRIST, Who is living,
The glory of JESU's Resurrection."

Second Mary :

"Bright angels attesting,
The shroud and napkin resting."

Third Mary :

"Yea, CHRIST my hope is arisen :
To Galilee He goes before you."

The Apostles act their scene of running to the sepulchre, and then, turning to the choir, sing,

"Happy they who hear the witness, Mary's word believing,
Above the tales of Jewry deceiving."

And the choir reply :

"CHRIST indeed from death is risen, our new life obtaining.
Have mercy, victor King, ever reigning !"

Finally, having got S. Mary Magdalene at the sepulchre, the trope-writers naturally make her meet the risen LORD there. Some thirteenth-century MSS. contain this addition, one of them having two appearances of our LORD, first *praeparatus in similitudinem hortulani*, and afterwards to all the women *in similitudinem Domini.*[1]

Not only were these additions appended to the trope, but it was sometimes prefaced by several stanzas of lamentations sung by the women on the way to the sepulchre, and these assisted in the linking-up process by carrying the thoughts of the hearers back to the events of Good Friday.

Another dialogue, representing the

[1] See the Orleans play in Wright, Davidson, and Pollard.

journey to Emmaus, is known to have formed part of the Easter Monday ceremonies at Lichfield towards the end of the twelfth century. Elsewhere, as at Beauvais, this theme was combined with that of the incredulity of S. Thomas. A play, extant at Tours, and dating from that century or the next, combines the soldiers keeping watch at the sepulchre, the *Quem queritis* in its most elaborate form and the Thomas episode, the whole ending with the *Te Deum*; which shows that even this long sequence of scenes was still only an interpolation, though doubtless a prominent and popular one, in divine service.

The eleventh-century tropers contain dialogues for Christmas and Ascension Day, of which the following will serve for specimens:

> "Quem queritis in praesepe, pastores, dicite."
> "Salvatorem Christum Dominum, infantem, pannis involutum secundum sermonem angelicum. Adest hic parvulus cum Maria matre sua," etc.

"Whom seek ye in the manger? shepherds, say."
"The Saviour, CHRIST the LORD, the Babe wrapped in swaddling clothes, according to the angel's word.
Lo, here is the Little One with Mary His mother."

"Quem cernitis ascendisse super astra, O Christicolae?"
"Iesum qui surrexit de sepulchro, O caelicolae."

"Whom have ye seen ascend above the stars, O ye followers of CHRIST?"
"JESUS Who rose from the sepulchre, O heavenly ones."

These are obviously imitations of the popular Easter trope, rather than the natural outcome of the services for their respective festivals. There is no scriptural authority for any such question addressed to the shepherds; and that attributed to the angels after the Ascension has been varied from the words of Acts i. 11, to bring it into harmony with the Easter form.

The effect of the Christmas tropes on

the history of the drama is of the highest importance. As the Easter tropes centre round the sepulchre, so these originate from the crib, which is still prominent in many churches at this season. A fourteenth century Rouen MS.[1] shows how the different parts of the church were made to represent various localities. The crib was behind the altar. The boy who took the angel's part was mounted *in excelso* before the choir. At the Epiphany the Magi were to come from different quarters and meet before the altar. After taking part in a procession they are warned by an angel not to return to Herod ; and the Mass begins, the play having served as Introit. The corresponding scene at Orleans[2] apparently took place at Mattins, being followed by the *Te Deum*.

Another trope of the Christmas season consisted of the lamentation of Rachel for her children, and her consolation by

[1] Davidson. [2] Wright, Davidson.

an angel. The three motives of the Shepherds, the Magi, and the Innocents are found in combination as early as the tenth century.[1] Herod's prominence in both the Innocents and Magi stories would help to connect them, and in this play we find him taking a leading part. It opens with a stage direction that he is to seat himself on his throne; and, once there, he quickly shows signs of the bluster and rant which were soon to make him a favourite character with the populace, and eventually a by-word for extravagant over-acting.[2] When the scribes tell him that CHRIST shall be born at Bethlehem, he drives them away in rage and hurls their book of prophecies after them. He quotes Sallust, and when his armour-bearer suggests the slaughter of the children, he cries, brandishing his

[1] The Freising play: Davidson.

[2] It is scarcely necessary, to refer to Hamlet's description of the inferior tragedian who "out-Herods Herod."—*Hamlet* III, ii.

sword, "Armiger eximie, pueros fac ense perire." The turgid bombast of the line is probably intentional. It is worth while noticing that in this armour-bearer we have an entirely non-scriptural personage, and in two midwives the first introduction of characters from the apocryphal books of the New Testament.

Another important source of the liturgical drama is to be found, not in any trope, but in the *lectio* which formed part of the Christmas offices, extracted from a famous sermon against Jews, infidels, and heretics, mistakenly ascribed to S. Augustine. In this various prophets are called upon to bear witness to Christ, and the answer of each is given from his writings. To the Jewish prophets are added Nebuchadnezzar, who saw in the furnace One like unto the Son of God, with Vergil and the Sibyl, both of whom were believed to have prophesied of Christ. The dramatic form of this reading led, by the eleventh century, to its being given in some places as a dialogue, a precentor questioning each of the prophets in turn.

Later versions (thirteenth and fourteenth centuries) show the inventive readiness which snatched at every opportunity for dramatic embellishment of the services. The prophets, each with his appropriate symbols, moved in procession up the church. In the nave a furnace with (presumably lighted) tow was set up, and the testimony of Nebuchadnezzar was expanded into a play of the Three Children. The presence of Balaam on his ass among the prophets furnished the excuse for grafting on another episodic drama. He is stopped by an angel, threatens the ass, and *puer sub asina respondet.* In the hands of persons determined at all costs to emphasize the dramatic side of divine worship in portraying the Bible story, such a process was capable of almost indefinite extension. It would not be difficult to place Noah

Plate 2.

Photo] [Tredov, Moscow.

PLAY OF THE THREE CHILDREN AT MOSCOW.
(See page 38.)

and Abraham among the prophets, and by bringing in the first Adam to testify to the second, the *Processus Prophetarum* might be made to lead back to the Creation.

Meanwhile other additions to the services were lengthening out the story in the opposite direction. Plays dealing with the lives of the saints not only provided additions to the services on the appropriate festivals, but also carried on the history of the Church after Pentecost. The thirteenth-century *Conversion of S. Paul*[1] and *Miracles of S. Nicholas*[2] indicate how large a field lay open to the dramatist in Holy Scripture and legend respectively.

Finally, the fact that in Advent the Church specially bears in mind the second coming of our LORD, gave opportunity to finish off the series, causing the line to stretch out, literally, to the crack of doom. The twelfth-century *Sponsus*[3]

[1] Wright. [2] Ibid. [3] Ibid.

takes the parable of the Ten Virgins as the basis of a liturgical drama suitable to the season. The foolish virgins lament their negligence in a series of Latin stanzas with the refrain in old French,

"Dolentas! chaitivas! trop i avem dormit."

"Alas, wretched ones! Too long have we slept."

In vain they appeal in turn to their wiser sisters, to the oil-merchants, and to the Bridegroom who pronounces their doom, after which, says the stage-direction, demons seize them and cast them into hell, a catastrophe which foreshadows an important and popular feature of the religious drama at a later period.

Another play of about the same date, the Tegernsee *Antichrist*,[1] deals with the end of the world in the manner of a great historical drama, if the expression may be used, when future events are in question.

[1] Wright, *Chester Plays*.

The kings of the earth are shown accepting the false Messiah who is destroyed in the moment of his triumph. The play is notable in various ways. It draws part of its material from the Book of Revelation, it includes abstractions such as Hypocrisy and Heresy among its characters, it requires an elaborate stage setting with *sedes* or thrones for the various kings, and it is the earliest religious drama of a political tendency, bearing, as it does, on the conflict of Frederick Barbarossa with Pope Alexander III.

Thus we have, at any rate *in posse*, the complete cycle. The Easter play, the germ of the whole, could be made to extend back to the Passion and forward to the Ascension and Whitsuntide. And this section would take its place in the more comprehensive growth of the Christmas plays, back to the Creation through the association of the prophets with the Nativity, and forward to the end of the world because the Advent services connected the second with the first coming of our LORD.

It is noteworthy that for a long time the liturgical drama forbore to give any actual representation of the Passion. It was content with the narration of it contained in the laments of the women as they approach the sepulchre,[1] and with the symbolism of the Deposition of the Cross. The gap was bridged by working into the cycle plays already in existence dealing with other episodes in the Gospels such as the raising of Lazarus, and the conversion of S. Mary Magdalene. These would help to link the events of Holy Week to the Easter plays in which the Magdalene was already a prominent figure. The first extant "Passion Play" proper is to be found in a thirteenth-century sequence of scenes written in Latin and German. It opens

[1] E.g., the stanzas beginning *Heu! pius pastor*, versions of which are printed by Frere, Chambers, and Pollard.

with the call of the Apostles and goes on to the entry into Jerusalem, the conversion of the Magdalene, the Betrayal, Passion, and Crucifixion.[1]

The liturgical drama reached its height about the middle of the thirteenth century. It could only develop further by cutting itself off from the Church services. Not only were the cycles of plays growing to an extent which made it inconvenient, if not impossible, that they should remain a mere incident of divine worship, but the very elements which offered the most promising possibilities of further development were those which were most alien and unsuitable to their liturgic purpose. Playwrights were ready enough to seize the possibilities of comedy which were latent in the homely talk of the shepherds or the bluster of Herod, and of drama in the repentance of the Magdalene or the sacrifice of Isaac. But to bring out their full effect it was necessary to free them

[1] See Chambers ii. 25.

from the hampering surroundings of a church and a form of service, and to establish them as independent dramas. Some of the factors in this process have already been noted, such as the tendency to embroider the scriptural narrative with new incidents, persons, and traits of character. None is more important than the adoption of the vernacular speech, which was indeed essential if the plays were to become popular entertainments. The only evidence for this in English liturgical drama is to be found in the fragments discovered by the late Professor Skeat, at Shrewsbury.[1] They contain portions of a Shepherds', a Resurrection, and an Emmaus play, and are written in English rhyme with Latin rubrics and texts interspersed.

The MS. has been attributed to the

[1] The discovery was announced in *The Academy*, January 4, 1890, and the text printed in the next number; it is also in Manly, and in *Non-cycle Mystery Plays*.

early years of the fifteenth century, but its contents were almost certainly composed much earlier, and are invaluable as illustrating the process of transition from liturgical to secular drama.

Scarcely less important was the change from singing and recitative to ordinary speech.. The Latin portions of the Shrewsbury plays are noted for voices, but the English dialogue was evidently intended to be spoken. When music and the Latin language were no longer essential to the plays their complete separation from the liturgy and the substitution of lay for clerical actors naturally followed.

Another reason for the separation is to be found in the elaborate "mounting" which had come into use. S. Aethelwold's impromptu sepulchre "in a vacant part of the altar" had been superseded by an elaborate and permanent structure. Many of the later plays require *sedes* representing different localities, the forerunners of the later scaffolds. In the

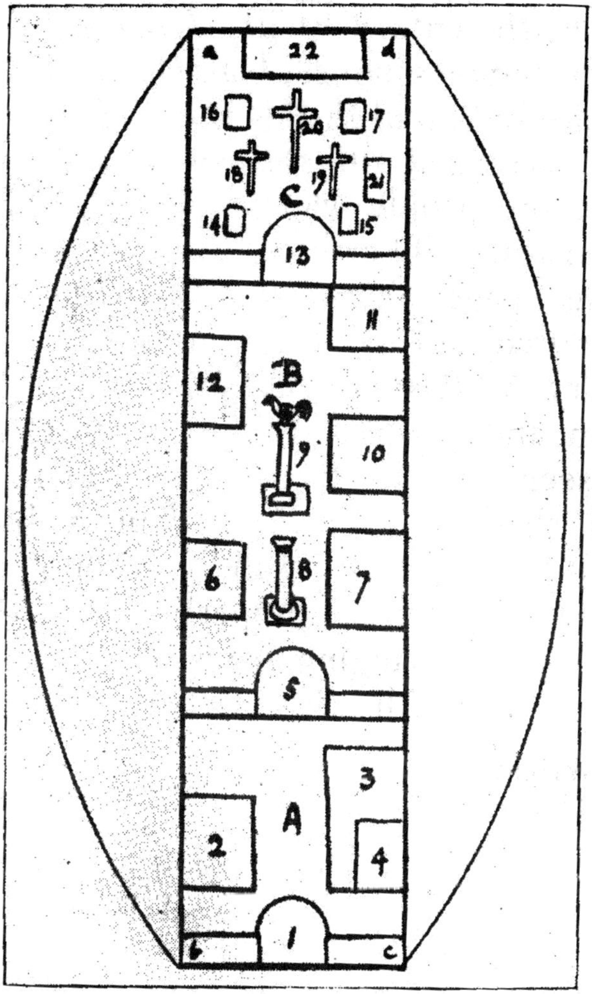

PLAN OF DONAUESCHINGEN PASSION PLAY STAGE.

Reproduced from E. K. Chambers's *Mediaeval Stage*, by permission of the Clarendon Press.

thirteenth-century Fleury *Lazarus*,[1] Jerusalem, Simon's house, Galilee,[2] and Bethany are indicated in this way. These *sedes* were arranged in the choir and nave, while the people watched the show from the aisles.[3] The illustration on the preceding page shows the arrangement of a church for a Passion Play. The Fleury *S. Paul*[4] demands, besides Jerusalem and Damascus, that Ananias shall be seen lying on a couch, and that Saul shall be let down "in a basket as if from the wall." Appropriate dresses, and stage properties, such as a moving star hanging from the roof, came into use. All this tendency towards

[1] Wright.

[2] Thought to have been represented by the west porch, which thus acquired the name of Galilee.

[3] Behind the altar in the fourteenth-century church of Tunstead, in Norfolk, is a stone platform about seven feet above the floor of the chancel. It has been conjectured that this was used as a stage for the performance of plays.

[4] Wright.

realism naturally assisted in the dissociation of the drama from the liturgy, while requirements of space suggested a move into the open air.

The century of transition (*c.* 1250–1350) from the purely liturgical period to complete separation will form the subject of the next chapter. Here it may be noted that the liturgical drama survived side by side with the later developments. The Digby MS. contains a fifteenth century Burial and Resurrection "to be playede, on part on gudfriday after-none, & the other part opon Ester-day." The first part consists chiefly of devotional lamentations spoken by Joseph of Arimathea and the holy women. One line, "O caluery! thy greyn colore is turnyd to rede," is a curious anticipation of Shakespeare. The second includes an English version of *Quem queritis*, and several Latin hymns, including the sequence *Victimae paschali*. It is in the sequence that the tropes left their most important and permanent mark upon the structure of the Mass. But the primitive Easter dialogue itself survived in some French churches until the eighteenth century.

The illustration opposite page 26 shows a Russian liturgical play of the Three Children, formerly performed in church, but recently revived in a secular building at Moscow. The Fiery Furnace occupies the middle of the stage, and the three children, wearing white fur caps and carrying candles, are touching the wings of the One like unto the Son of Man. Beside the furnace kneel two men dressed as characters in the play and holding palms. The other figures are in the ordinary dress of a Russian Cathedral choir.

CHAPTER III

The Stage moves out of Church

SOME of the earliest indications of the coming separation of liturgy and drama are to be found in the plays of Hilarius, the first writer of this kind to whom we can assign a name and an individual existence. We know little more of him than that he is believed to have been born in England, that he flourished in the first half of the twelfth century, and was a disciple of Abelard. His *Daniel*, which may well be an elaborated excrescence on a *Processus Prophetarum*, is in two parts, telling respectively the stories of the prophet at Belshazzar's feast and in the lions' den. Both this play and his *Raising of Lazarus* close with a direction that if it is performed at Mattins the *Te Deum* is to be sung, if at Vespers the

Magnificat. This is significant of the loosening of the tie between drama and liturgy. The play no longer grows naturally out of a particular act of worship, but is written independently, and may be attached to any service. The third extant drama of Hilarius bears no indication of any such attachment. It is a frankly comic version of a miracle of S. Nicholas[1] written in rhyming Latin with French refrains, which are also a feature of his *Lazarus*. The hero, though a heathen, entrusts his goods when he is about to start on a journey, to an image of S. Nicholas. Returning, he finds them stolen, and upbraids the image in brisk verse, of which a specimen may be given:

> "Gravis sors et dura!
> Hic reliqui plura,
> Sed sub mala cura.
> *Des! quel domage!*
> *Qui pert la sue chose purque n'enrage.*

[1] Pollard.

Hic res plusquam centum
Misi et argentum ;
Sed non est inventum.
Des ! quel domage !
Qui pert la sue chose purque n'enrage."

"Here 's a pretty mess indeed !
I trusted all my goods at need
To one who paid them little heed.
Zounds ! To be robbed in this fashion !
Would throw any man into a passion.

Valuables, above five score,
Here I left, with coin galore ;
But I shall never see them more.
Zounds ! To be robbed in this fashion !
Would throw any man into a passion."

He then proceeds to cudgel the defaulting image, with the result that the indignant saint appears in person, and prevails on the robbers to restore their booty by the simple expedient of threatening them with public exposure ; whereupon the grateful heathen is converted. It is a mere anecdote told in a hundred and twenty short lines, but it is notable as the first outcome of the liturgical drama, which is purely comic in intention. The comparatively large number of extant S. Nicholas plays[1] (though none is so lively as that of Hilarius) suggests that the festival of this popular saint was regarded as a specially appropriate time for these "breakings out of mirth." And the fact that the "Boy Bishop" was elected on S. Nicholas' Day supplies a link between this kind of drama and the midwinter revellings to be mentioned below.

Further evidence for the existence of saints' plays independent of the scriptural cycles is to be found in the story of Abbot Geoffrey of St. Albans, who, while a schoolmaster at Dunstable, wrote a play of S. Katharine, "of the kind we commonly call miracles," says Matthew Paris in telling the story.[2] For

[1] Wright prints a group of four from a thirteenth-century MS.

[2] *Gesta Abbatum Monasterii Sancti Albani*, i. 73. Rolls Series.

its performance he borrowed some copes from the Abbey of St. Albans, which were burnt while in his possession, whereupon, as an act of reparation, he became a monk in the abbey, and in 1119 was elected abbot. We may therefore fix the date of his play at about 1100. From William FitzStephen's *Life of Becket*[1] we learn that plays "representing the miracles wrought by holy confessors, or the glorious sufferings of the steadfast martyrs," were common in twelfth century London. Though such spectacles were doubtless given in honour of particular saints, and on their festivals, they no longer formed part of the services, nor were they necessarily acted in church, but in some neighbouring place, such as the churchyard.

The absence of any evidence of such independent plays in England before the Norman Conquest, together with the

[1] *Materials for the History of Thomas Becket*, iii. 9. Rolls Series.

appearance of Geoffrey's *S. Katharine*, about a generation after that event, suggests that they were an importation from abroad. This conclusion is strengthened by the twelfth-century Norman play of *Adam*, which is a development of a section of the liturgical cycle, but designed to be played independently and in the open air.

The MS. directs that "A Paradise is to be made in a raised spot, with curtains and cloths of silk hung round it at such a height that persons in the Paradise may be visible from the shoulders upwards. Fragrant flowers and leaves are to be set round about, and divers trees put therein with hanging fruit, so as to give the likeness of a most delicate spot."[1]

The Creator is to be clad in a dalmatic, Adam in a red tunic, and Eve in white. After the first dialogue the Creator departs into the church, which represents heaven. The only other

[1] Chambers, ii. 80.

characters in this scene are the demons who run about outside Paradise, and at one point "make a sally amongst the people." After the Fall, Adam and Eve, wearing "poor raiment sewn together with fig-leaves," till the ground. The devil sows thorns and thistles in it, and at last leads them off to hell, where his companions "make a great smoke arise, and call aloud to each other with glee in their hell, and clash their pots and kettles that they may be heard without." The same fate awaits Cain and Abel at the end of their scene, which is followed by a *Processus Prophetarum*, each prophet in turn being dragged off to hell.

Another instance of the custom of acting plays in the open is found in a thirteenth-century Appendix to the *Life of S. John of Beverley*, which records the miraculous cure of a boy who had fallen from the rood-loft of Beverley church while a play of the Resurrection was being performed "according to custom" in the churchyard. He had climbed up in order to see through the windows, over the heads of the crowd which had been drawn together by various motives—wonder, devotion, or the pursuit of pleasure.[1] The direction in the thirteenth-century Orleans Nativity Play mentioned above,[2] that the crib is to be set up "at the gates of the monastery," suggests that part, at any rate, of the action was to pass in the open, though the play was apparently still associated with a choir office. The plays referred to in a Latin story of the same period must have been quite detached from the Church services. It tells how two friars, coming upon a large crowd assembled in a meadow in silence broken by bursts of applause and laughter, conclude that "spectacles such as we are wont to call miracles" are being performed.[3]

[1] *Historians of the Church of York*, i. 328. Rolls Series.
[2] Above, p. 23.
[3] Wright, *Latin Stories*, p. 100.

As a rule the sacred drama has been employed for the edification of the faithful rather than as a missionary agency for the conversion of the heathen. But that its possibilities in this respect were not overlooked at this period is seen from the story of the German missionaries who performed a play before the heathen Livonians at Riga in 1204, when "the spectators, interpreting the scenes more literally than their instructors intended, fled in terror at the sight of the Midianites attacked by Gideon's army, and imagined that the next assault would be directed against themselves." [1]

As soon as the plays began to free themselves from the limitations imposed by their original position in the liturgy, it was natural that scholars like Hilarius should take them in hand with a view to drawing out their literary possibilities.

From the fact that Geoffrey was a schoolmaster it is not very audacious

[1] Maclear, *History of Missions*, p. 238.

to infer that his *S. Katharine* was intended for representation by his pupils. Dramatic performances on more or less classical lines are a perennial feature of school festivals. But, though there is evidence of such performances during the Middle Ages, the drama in general was but slightly affected by classical influences, and retained, at any rate until the sixteenth century, the form it had received during its liturgical period.

Of the purely comic side there is a very different story to tell. So long as the drama was strictly confined to the liturgy the appetite of the natural man for foolery could only find vent in secular festivities. Chief among these were the revels, with which, ever since pagan times, midwinter and the incoming of the New Year were celebrated. By the tenth century the Church began to imitate them with similar festivities of its own. The most famous of these, the "Feast of Fools," is not found until the twelfth century. It began at Vespers on the last day of the year. A subdeacon was chosen lord of the feast, and at the verse in the *Magnificat*, *Deposuit de sede potentes et exaltavit humiles*, he took the place of the precentor, other subdeacons occupied the canons' stalls, and the feast was celebrated with riotous revelling and much mock ritual.

A similar feast was that of the "Boy Bishop," who was chosen by the choir-boys on S. Nicholas' Day (December 6th), and on Innocents' Day took the place of the real bishop and ruled the Church until the *Deposuit* verse came round next day, when he in turn was deposed. This custom was more popular in England than the "Feast of Fools," which flourished principally in the cathedral towns of France. Boy bishops continued to be chosen here until 1542. They were revived under Mary, and again abolished at the accession of Elizabeth. Such customs reacted on the religious drama in encouraging both the tendency towards make-believe and impersonation and also the introduction of extraneous matter and revelling into the services.

Another opportunity was given by the "Feast of the Ass," which was directly connected with the liturgical drama through the presence of Balaam's ass in the *Prophetae*, and the association of the animal with the flight into Egypt, and with the Palm Sunday procession. We learn from a twelfth-century MS. that this Feast was celebrated at Beauvais on January 14th. A procession representing the flight into Egypt was brought into church with much drinking and revelling. A rollicking hymn [1] in praise of the ass was sung, and imitations of braying were interpolated at various points in the Mass, the *Ite missa est*, for example,

[1] The tune is the well-known *Orientis Partibus*, which is given with the melody of the refrain (*Benedicite*) in the *English Hymnal*, 129.

giving way to a threefold "*Hin-Han*," to which the congregation made a similar response.

Such excesses naturally drew down the rebukes of those in authority. In 1207 Pope Innocent III formally prohibited maskings and other debauchery in church. This decree appears to have referred rather to such revels as have just been described than to the acting of plays.[1] But as time went on the plays themselves came to be regarded with suspicion. The *Handlyng Synne*, a poem of 1303, draws a distinction between playing the Resurrection or the Nativity in church, "to make men to beleue stedfastly," and acting miracles on highways or greens, which is sinful. The Church had encouraged the earlier developments of the plays in order that they might supply a more powerful counter-attraction to the obscenities of the secular revels. But the

[1] For the survival of the practice of acting plays in church see below, p. 88, and note.

tendency to elaborate their attractive features at the expense of their devotional and didactic side grew apace as soon as they were removed from their original place in the liturgy, and eventually resulted in their complete emancipation from clerical control.

The Parish Clerks of London, a semi-religious corporation, long maintained the custom of performing scriptural plays at Skinner's Well (Clerkenwell). In 1391 they played a three-day cycle before the king and queen, and in 1409 one which lasted eight days and was attended "by the most part of the nobility and gentry of England."[1] About 1378 the scholars and choristers of S. Paul's were still acting Christmas plays, apparently in the open air.

But these fragmentary survivals from the purely ecclesiastical period of dra-

[1] Stow, *Survey of London*, ed. C. L. Kingsford, i. 15. See also Grey Friars Chronicle in *Monumenta Franciscana*, ii. 164. Rolls Series.

Plate 4.

BRUGES PROCESSION.
CHRIST AND THE DOCTORS.
(See page 155.)

matic history are overshadowed after the beginning of the fourteenth century by the results of the entrance into the story of the "guilds" or corporations of the members of particular trades in each city. These guilds played an important part in municipal affairs in the Middle Ages. Their co-operation in the drama may apparently be traced to the custom of celebrating great events, such as a royal visit, or anniversaries, such as May Day, by a "riding" or procession in which the guilds took part.

Processions were also a feature of ecclesiastical celebrations. And the step which associated the two was taken in 1311, when Pope Clement V made the feast of Corpus Christi one of universal obligation. Then was instituted the great Corpus Christi procession of the Host in which laity as well as clergy took part. Before long the custom arose that each craft should contribute to it a group, allegorical or otherwise, which rode

Plate 5.

Furnes Procession—Nativity Tableau.
(See page 155.)

through the streets or was drawn on a car. These were called "pageants," and were designed to represent scriptural incidents appropriate to the several guilds. At first the representation was merely in dumb-show. As soon as it was desired to proceed to speech or action, it became necessary that halts should be made for the purpose. In this way another outlet was provided for the growing energies of the religious drama. The clergy, who had hitherto retained it in their own hands, now joined forces with the guilds, and this combination produced the great miracle cycles which are described in the following chapter.

The sketch that has here been given of the growth of the drama up to this point has not been confined to England, both because the materials are so fragmentary that we must needs take our evidence where we can find it, and also because the plays grew up under the auspices of the Church as a whole, and local variations are comparatively unimportant. But the English miracle cycles with which we have now to deal form in themselves a complete body of literature, and it would be altogether outside the scope of so small a work as the present to attempt any comparison of them with the contemporary plays of other countries. In France such plays are known as *mystères*. The corresponding word "mystery" was introduced into English literature by eighteenth and nineteenth century writers, who applied it to plays dealing with New Testament subjects, confining the term "miracle" to those based on legends of the saints. In mediaeval England no such distinction was known. The word "miracle," a shortened form of *repraesentatio miraculi*, though it may well have taken its origin from the saints' plays referred to in this chapter, was commonly used to describe any kind of religious play.

CHAPTER IV

The Miracle Plays

THE establishment of the Feast of Corpus Christi in 1311 led directly to the golden age of the religious drama in England. Within a generation or so the great miracle cycles had come to maturity in the hands of the guilds. And for more than two centuries miracle plays fill a large space in the life and thought of the English people. It will be the object of this chapter to present a summary view of this period treated as a whole.

Five complete cycles and a number of smaller groups and single plays have survived. The manuscript of the forty-eight York plays dates from about 1430–40, but the plays themselves were

Plate 6.

Humorous Sketch of Fourteenth-century Pageant and Spectators (from MS. Bodley, 264).

(See page 81.)

probably written about 1350. Many of them show the miracle in its simplest form, little developed from the liturgical period. Others introduce the comic element, as in the quarrel between Noah and his wife, who is reluctant to enter the ark.[1] The Passion gives opportunity for some horrid realism. Several incidents are taken from the apocryphal Gospel of Nicodemus. One of these supplies the germ of a character, Pilate's Beadle, of whom much is made. He rebukes his master for kissing his wife in court, puts him to bed on the stage, and has difficulty in rousing him when the Jews arrive. Other original characters are the honest porter, who bluntly expresses his suspicions of Judas, and the squire who leases Calvary to the Jews and

[1] This incident is common to most of the cycles. Chaucer mentions as a well-known fact :

"The sorwe of Noe with his felaweshipe
Er that he myghte brynge his wyf to shipe."
Cant. Tales, Miller's Tale.

is cheated by them. But the prevailing note is a simple and devotional following of the Bible story, rising to real beauty in the Virgin's worship of her Infant:

"Hayle my lord God! hayle prince of pees!
Hayle my fadir, and hayle my sone!

. . . .

O nowe slepis my sone, blist mot he be;
And lyes full warme ther bestis by-twene."

The twenty-four Chester plays are extant only in versions written about the end of the sixteenth century.[1] But the form in which this, like other cycles, has survived is clearly the growth of centuries, and not the work of any one writer. Traces of its liturgical origin are embedded in the Ascension Play, while the lament of the women at the Cross strikes a comparatively modern note:

"Come downe, Lorde, and breake thy bandes,
Lose and heale thy lovelye handes."

[1] In the MS. of 1592 each play is signed (with slight variations) "*Finis! Deo gratias! per me, Georgi Bellin*, 1592. Come, LORD JESU; come quicklye."

This cycle shows the plays in a more elaborate stage than that of York. An Antichrist play is inserted; the Sybil is borrowed from the *Prophetae* and given a scene with the Emperor Octavian. The *Prophetae* also contribute Balaam and his ass, the stage-direction *loquetur aliquis in asina* suggesting a sort of pantomime donkey. Other opportunities are taken for the introduction of irrelevant comic matter; for instance, the episode of the dishonest ale-wife, who is left in hell when the other souls are delivered.

The inevitable outcome of this tendency is seen in the cycle variously named from the Towneley family, original possessors of the fifteenth century manuscript, from Wakefield, where it was performed, and from Woodkirk, its traditional place of origin. It consists of thirty-two plays, some of which are based on those of York or on a common original. But a group of about eight, believed to be the work of a single writer of the early fifteenth century, shows the miracle drama at the height of its literary, dramatic, and comic power.

Such a writer naturally develops those possibilities in the plays which lend themselves to the exercise of his talents, without always considering the effect on the original tendency and proportion of the story. In the Passion scenes his grotesque and powerful realism is very effective. Nothing in the entire series is more striking than the paroxysms of fury and malice into which Caiaphas is thrown by our LORD's silence, which, in another play, is contrasted with the grim professional talk of the executioners as they nail Him to the Cross. The Crucifixion is followed by a grotesque piece of comic relief in which the executioners wrangle and throw dice for our LORD's garments with Pilate, whose conventional brag in this writer's hands takes a more literary form than usual :—

Plate 7.

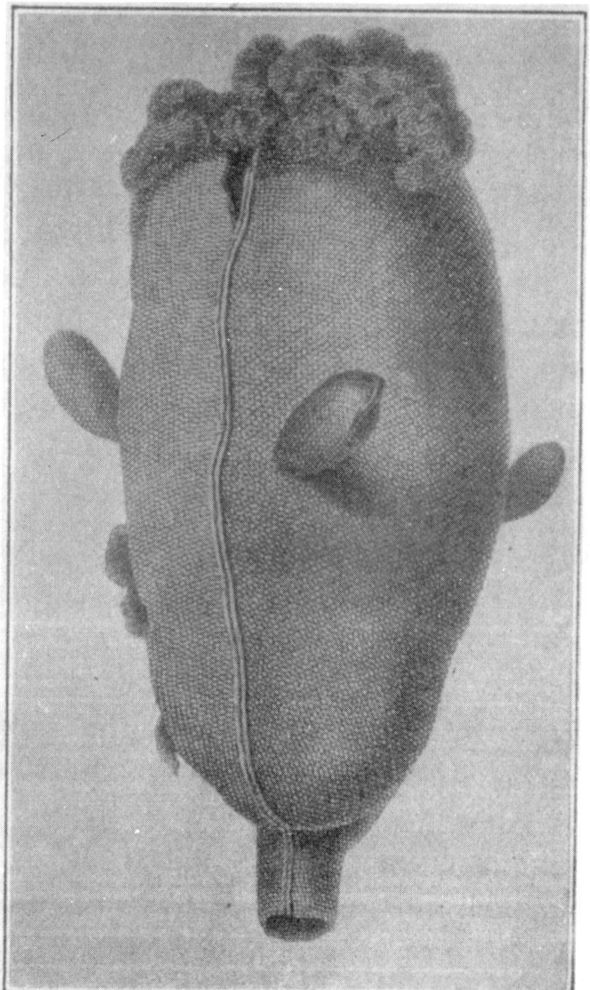

HEAD OF PILATE'S CLUB
(from T. Sharp's *Dissertation on Pageants*).
(See page 87.)

"Stynt, I say, gyf men place, quia sum dominus dominorum,
He that agans me says rapietur lux oculorum,
Therfor gyf ye me space, ne tendam vim brachiorum,
And then get ye no grace, contestor Iura polorum."

But he plays a despicable part, first trying to bounce them out of the clothes, and then begging the prize from the winner.

A vivid but somewhat irrelevant piece of satire is introduced into the Last Judgement, the devils discussing the sins of the time which keep hell's porter busy "up erly and downe late." More to the purpose is their horrible gloating over their victims after the Judgement. But by common consent the top of "the Wakefield master's" achievement is the *Secunda Pastorum*, or second of the two Shepherds' Plays in this series. He follows up the homely dialogue with which it was customary to introduce this episode with the entrance of one Mak, who makes off with a sheep. This leads to a genuinely comic scene in Mak's cottage, where the thief and his wife seek to escape detection by hiding the sheep in the cradle and passing it off as their child. The writer may have intended a subtle foreshadowing of the scene in the stable at Bethlehem, which was to close the play, though no doubt it was the farcical humour of the interpolation that chiefly appealed to his audience. But the simple beauty of the addresses with which the shepherds present their gifts in the last scene wipes out all other impressions. Nothing could be more effective than the First Shepherd's sudden change from fierce exultation over the defeat of the Evil One to delight in the Infant's smile :

> "Lo, he merys ;
> Lo, he laghys, my swetyng,
> A welfare metyng,
> I have holden my hetyng,[1]
> Have a bob of cherys."

[1] promise.

The Third Shepherd's stanza also deserves quotation :

"Haylle, derlyng dere, full of godhede,
I pray the be nere when that I have nede.
Haylle ! swete is thy chere : my hart wold blede
To se the sytt here in so poore wede,
With no pennys.
Haylle ! put furthe thy dalle,[1]
I bryng the bot[2] a balle :
Have and play the with alle,
And go to the tenys."

The Cornish plays composed in the fourteenth or fifteenth century differ considerably in structure and tone from the English cycles. They introduce subjects not found elsewhere, such as the building of the Temple and the death of Pilate ; but their general affect is one of greater homogeneity, and they make few efforts after extraneous comic or dramatic effect.

The so-called "Coventry plays," or *Ludus Coventriae*, present several features

[1] fist. [2] but.

of interest. The tradition which says that they were acted by the Grey Friars of Coventry cannot now be accepted. Nor is there any evidence to connect them with the trade guilds. A prologue announces,

> "A Sunday next, yf that we may,
> At vj of the belle we gynne our play,
> In N. towne."

From this it has been inferred that they were performed by strolling players, N. (nomen) signifying that the name of any town might be inserted as required. It has also been thought to stand for Norwich, Northampton, or some other town of the East Midlands, where the language of the plays shows them to have originated. The theory which associates them with a religious order derives plausibility, however, from the large admixture of mediaeval theology which distinguishes them. Seven of the forty-two plays are taken up with the birth, early life, and marriage of the Blessed

Virgin related in a devotional spirit with much interpolation of psalms and hymns. So in the scene of CHRIST in the Temple the Holy Child does not merely recite the Commandments as in some other versions, but discusses abstruse questions with the doctors. He thus illustrates the Incarnation:

> "Lyke as the sunne doth pers[1] the glas,
> The glas not hurte of his nature,
> Ryght so the Godhede entryd has
> The virgynes wombe, and sche mayd pure."

Another feature of the cycle is the inclusion of abstractions among the characters. "Contemplacio" introduces some of the episodes, and the Annunciation is preceded by a dialogue of the Heavenly Virtues.[2] The tendency throughout is to give prominence to what makes for edification and devotion, eschewing the grotesque and comic, except for occasional touches, as when the Jews

[1] pierce. [2] See above, p. 7.

"dawncyn abowte the cros," or the trial of Joseph and Mary is made the occasion for a satire on the church courts.

The surviving texts also include several plays which formed part of similar cycles now lost,[1] and a number of single plays, such as the *S. Paul*, and *S. Mary Magdalene* preserved in the Digby MS., which were presumably performed on the appropriate festivals, and never formed part of any cycles.

From the brief analysis of the complete cycles given above it will be seen that, in spite of differences in tone, they all retain the general form and outline which they received in the fourteenth century from their original purpose of setting forth, for

[1] For instance two plays have survived from a lost Coventry guild cycle, which seems to have differed from the extant ones in beginning with the Annunciation, and consisting of only ten pageants. This cycle must be distinguished from the *Ludus Coventriae* described above, which is associated with Coventry only by an apparently erroneous tradition.

the edification of beholders, the Divine Plan of Redemption. The fall of Lucifer serves for prologue and gives occasion for the creation of man, whose fall in turn the devil is induced to seek through envy. Other Old Testament subjects are for the most part developed from the *Processus Prophetarum* and restricted to those which can be brought into the general plan by supplying types of CHRIST or of the Church, such as Abel, the Ark, the sacrifice of Isaac, the Exodus. From these we pass to the group, extending from the Annunciation to CHRIST in the Temple, of which the germ was the Christmas trope. The Baptism and Temptation of our LORD are a necessary part of the scheme, and we then pass over the intervening ministry to the events of Holy Week and Easter. To this group, which finds its origin in the *Quem queritis*, the Ascension and Pentecost also belong; and the Last Judgement crowns the whole.

Few departures from this order are found in the great cycles. The York plays bring in the Transfiguration and a group of plays dealing with the Assumption of the Blessed Virgin. This subject also occurs in the *Ludus Coventriae*, and Chester has an Antichrist play. Three cycles introduce the woman taken in adultery, and four the raising of Lazarus, which, as suggested above,[1] may be considered as almost part of the Holy Week and Easter group. But even in these earlier cycles we see the tendency to depart in spirit if not in form from the original purpose of the plays, by working up the dramatic, pathetic, or comic opportunities of their subjects.

Some instances of this have already been given. To them may be added the Sacrifice of Isaac, which clearly afforded most promising opportunities of drama and pathos. Of these the Chester play-

[1] See p. 31.

wright makes skilful use in bringing out the anguish of the father and terror of the son, combined with the dutiful submission of both to the Divine Will. In other versions of this situation the agony is drawn out with still more conscious art.[1]

The Towneley sheep-stealing farce is the most notable example of the comic interpolation. But there is also a tendency to assimilate scriptural personages to the stock types of comedy. Thus Noah becomes the conventional comic husband henpecked by a shrewish wife; Cain the stupid master who is the butt of an impudent servant. Even S. Joseph approximates to the stock figure of the old bachelor married to a young wife.

In the fifteenth century we find playwrights deliberately working up the popular elements. Prominent among these was the devil, and so he is introduced into the Newcastle play of the "Building of the Ark," tempting Noah's

[1] See the so-called "Dublin" and Brome plays.

wife to oppose her husband, swearing "by my crooked snout," and winding-up with a comical threat addressed to the spectators.

Similarly the fifteenth century Digby *S. Paul* drags in a scene in hell simply to show Belial and his messenger "Marcury" raging over Saul's conversion, after which "thei shal vanyshe away with a fyrye flame and a tempest." The *Mary Magdalene*[1] of the same group has a similar scene in which the devils expelled from the heroine, "enter into hell with thondyr," and are tried and beaten for their failure.

Another popular feature was the bragging, ranting ruler, causing roars of laughter by his extravagant claims,[2] by his threats against disrespectful spectators,

[1] More fully discussed below. See p. 106.

[2] "Bothe of hevyn and of herthe I am kynge," says Herod in the *Ludus Coventriae*: and in the Coventry guild play he declares that he "made bothe hevin and hell."

HEROD IN A SIXTEENTH-CENTURY GERMAN PLAY.
(After an old Original at the Royal Staatsbibliothek, Munich.)

and by allusions to his personal beauty. Here the joke lay in his being made up as a hideous worshipper of Mahownd, who ranks with "Sir Satan" and Lucifer as the tutelary deity of all non-Christians, Pharaoh, Herod, Pilate, or Tiberius. Among the accomplishments of "Joly Absolon" the parish clerk Chaucer mentions that—

> "Sometyme to shewe his lightnesse and maistrye
> He pleyeth Herodes on a scaffold hye."[1]

A stage direction in the Coventry Shearmen's play shows the opportunities which the character afforded for extravagant "business." "Here Erode ragis in the pagond (i.e., on the stage) and in the strete also." These popular features were soon extended to Pilate and other potentates.[2] Finally the Digby *Massacre*

[1] *Cant. Tales*, Miller's Tale.

[2] Chaucer likens the bellowing of his drunken miller to "Pilate's voys."

The York Pilate boasts among other things of his descent from "Sir Seisar" [Caesar], and explains that *of the Innocents* gives Herod a foil, one Watkyn, a cowardly braggart of the usual *miles gloriosus* type, who is ignominiously routed by the mothers, the pathos of the scene being slurred over for the sake of this comic effect.

When the original offered no plausible opportunity for the introduction of comic scenes they were brought in with little or no excuse. Instances of this are the dialogue between Saul's servant and the ostler in the Digby *S. Paul*, and the episode of the quack doctor and his man in the Croxton *Play of the Sacrament*.

This play also illustrates another tendency of the latter portion of the period under consideration, the striving after sensational stage effects. It is a version

he was called Pilate because his mother was Pila and her father Atus; a piece of etymology which recalls Mr. Boffin's derivation of his wife's name, "Henerietty Boffin—which her Father's name was Henery, and her mother's name was Hetty, and so you get it."—*Our Mutual Friend*, ch. v.

of the well-known legend in which a Jew gets possession of a consecrated Host and tortures it. Here the self-introductory "boast," as it was technically called, is extended to "Sir Jonathas the Jew," who afterwards runs mad on finding he cannot detach the Host from his hand; his friends come to his rescue, but only succeed in pulling his arm off. Sensation is piled on sensation's head. The Host bleeds when stabbed. They boil it, and blood appears in the cauldron. Finally they bake it when "the ovyn must ryve asunder & blede owt at the cranys [cracks], & an image appere owt with woundis bledyng." The Digby *Mary Magdalene* contains a house on fire, a mock sacrifice to Mahownd, and various allegorical spectacles. As late as 1584 the Smiths of Coventry produced an entirely new play of the Destruction of Jerusalem, a subject quite inappropriate to the cycle into which it was introduced, but chosen apparently because of the opportunities it afforded for melodramatic spectacle.

We turn now from the plays themselves to the manner of their representation. In course of time they became too long and too important for their original position as "stations," or halts, in the Corpus Christi procession, and had to be separated from it. Thus at York from 1426 they were given on the day before Corpus Christi, the procession keeping its place on the feast itself. But the performances still retained the character derived from their processional origin, as is shown by Archdeacon Rogers's account of the Chester plays, written near the end of the sixteenth century :

"The manner of which playes was thus : they weare divided into 24 pagiantes, according to the companyes of the cittie, and every companye brought forthe their pagiant, which was the cariage or place which the [they] played in. And thei first beganne at the Abbaye gates ; and when the firste pagiante was played at the Abbaye gates, then it was wheeled from thense to Pentice, at the hyghe crosse, before

Plate 9.

HUMOROUS SKETCH OF FOURTEENTH-CENTURY PAGEANT AND SPECTATORS
(from MS. Bodley, 264).
(See page 81.)

the maior, and before that was donne the seconde came, and the first went into the Watergate Streete, and from thense unto the Bridge Streete, and so one after an other till all the pagiantes weare played appoynted for the firste daye, and so likewise for the seconde and the thirde daye. These pagiantes or cariges was a highe place made like a howse, with 2 rowmes, beinge open on the tope ; the lower rowme theie apparrelled and dressed themselves, and the higher rowme thei played ; and thei stoode upon vi [1] wheeles ; and when the [they] had donne with one cariage in one place, thei wheled the same from one streete to another."

At York the normal number of these stations or halting-places was twelve. At Coventry there were only three or four ; at Beverley, in 1449, six. The "pageants" were elaborate and permanent structures, sometimes built in special shapes appropriate to the scene to be represented. Thus Noah's pageant would be shaped like an ark, and "Hell," towards the end of the period if not before, was represented with an enormous

[1] In another version, iv.

mouth opening on the ground, whence flames and weird noises proceeded, and the devils ran in and out among the spectators to their mingled terror and delight. Sometimes the pageants were roofed over in order that such scenes as the Ascension might be represented, or our LORD descending to Judgement "in a cloud if it can be done," says the Chester play. The ground in front formed part of the stage, and the characters descended to it by means of ladders, e.g., when a journey was to be represented. The Chester play of the Magi has the direction, "Then the kinges goe downe to the beastes and ryde aboute."

Another pageant of this cycle is accompanied and explained by an expositor on horseback, who at the end rides off with it, crying,

> "Make rombe, lordinges, and geve us waye,
> And let Balacke come in and plaie."

But the plays were not always given in this peripatetic style. Sometimes the whole cycle was performed on one spot, such as the market-place, round which a number of scaffolds were erected to represent different scenes. These are a development of the *sedes* of the liturgical plays. We read of Pilate on his scaffold, Herod on his, and the characters pass and repass ; or the centre of interest shifts as one scene succeeds another. The stage-directions of the *Ludus Coventriae* illustrate this, and also show that the pageants might have curtains :

> " Here Cryst entereth into the hous with his disciplis and ete the Paschal lomb ; and in the mene tyme the cownsel-hous beforn-seyd xal sodeynly onclose, schewyng the buschopys, prestys and jewgys sytting in here [their] astat [state], lyche as it were a convocacyon."

In the fifteenth-century French miniature of the martyrdom of S. Apollonia the central space is occupied by the principal scene, and the spectators are standing under the surrounding scaffolds, among which Heaven and Hell can be identified.

Apparently the two methods might be combined by the erection, at each halting-place, of fixed scaffolds to serve as subsidiary stages, the movable pageant being brought in as a centrepiece. In any case the performers must have relied on the willingness of the spectators to bring a good deal of imagination to bear on very rudimentary stage arrangements and conventions.

When the sea was to be represented, a hole might be dug in the ground before the pageant, and filled with water on which floated a little boat; or, if the circular stage described below[1] was employed, the ditch which surrounded it might be made to contain enough water to carry such a boat from one scaffold to another.

Some of the elaborate stage effects attempted in the fifteenth century have

[1] P. 105. The Cornish plays were performed on stages of this kind. The amphitheatres at St. Just and Perranzabulo were about 130 feet in diameter.

Plate 10.

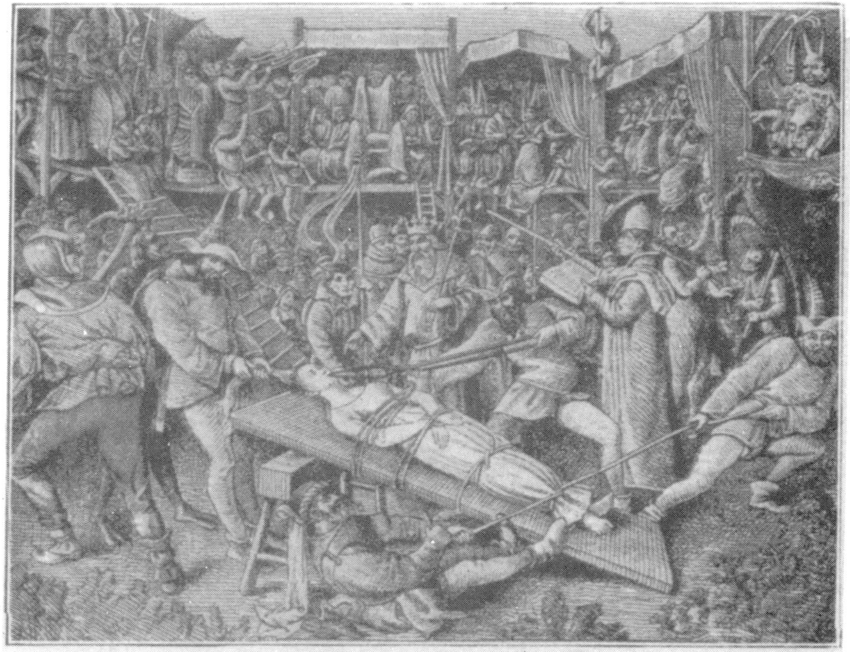

MARTYRDOM OF S. APOLLONIA

(a French Fifteenth-century Miniature, from *Essai sur l'histoire du Théatre*, published by Hachette et Cie, Paris). (See page 83.)

already been noticed. In the earlier cycles stage properties and effects were few and simple. The Chester Noah and his family recite a catalogue of the animals entering the Ark, which was "borded round about and one [on] the bordes all the beastes and foules painted. The "drombodaries" on which the Chester Magi ride, "for sweifter beastes be their non," were probably of the nature of hobby-horses. The Towneley Exodus directs that the Egyptians are to be overwhelmed by the sea, but gives no hint how this was to be done. Here too a good deal was probably left to the imagination.

In matters of costume and make-up convention was the ruling factor. The devil was to be as grotesque as possible. The Chester "Banes" or prologue describes him "in his fethers all ragger and rente." And the Newcastle reference to his "crooked snout" implies a mask. We read in the account books of wings for angels, a "tayle for ye serpente," wigs, gloves, and so on. The shepherds at Chester describe S. Joseph as having "a pound of heaire about his mouth and more." Herod carried a painted sword, which the Chester stage directions bid him "caste downe" and eventually "breake" in his rage, and Pilate a club of leather stuffed with wool, an instrument probably of much knockabout fun.

As regards the organization in general, some attempt was made to entrust each guild with a play appropriate to it. Thus the Water-drawers would take the "Flood," the Bakers the "Last Supper," the Cooks the "Harrowing of Hell," because they were always taking things out of the fire! Some rich guild, the Goldsmiths or the Mercers, would be required to present the Magi with becoming magnificence. Sometimes the choice would be determined by the association of a guild with a particular saint; the Barbers of Beverley played the Baptism of CHRIST in honour of their patron S. John Baptist. At

Lincoln in 1483 the Dean and Chapter took their share as a guild, and contributed the Assumption of our Lady, played not on a scaffold but in the nave of the cathedral, presumably as the climax of a cycle.[1]

Sometimes two or more guilds combined to contribute a play or group of plays. Others sought to evade their obligations. The texts afford evidence of the division and combination of the plays to suit the varying number of the guilds. The arrangements were in the hands of the town authorities, who had power to punish shortcomings. In 1452, one Cowper, a weaver of Beverley, was fined 6*s.* 8*d.* for not knowing his part,

[1] The practice of performing plays in churches survived into the sixteenth century. It is forbidden by Bishop Bonner's injunctions of 1542 (Wilkins *Concilia* iii. 866). The last official utterance of the Church on the subject is Canon 88 of 1604, which bids the churchwardens "suffer no Playes . . . or any other prophane usage to be kept in the Church, Chappell, or Churchyard."

an amount afterwards reduced to 4*d.* on account of his poverty. In 1521 the Beverley painters were fined 3*s.* for bringing contempt on the town by their bad and confused performance.

The guilds themselves levied "pagent pencys," each member paying from 1*d.* to 1*s.* to meet expenses. These consisted of the provision of the pageant itself, dresses and properties, e.g. "a new hoke to hange Judas, vj*d.*" and miscellaneous items, from the arrangement of such a spectacle as setting the world on fire (at the Day of Judgement) to 1*d.* for "sope to grese the wheles" of the pageant.

The performers also must be paid for their trouble. In the Norwich Grocers' play the representative of the Creator received 1*s.* 4*d.*, Adam, 6*d.*, Eve, the serpent, and the angel, 4*d.* each. At Coventry such popular characters as Herod, Pilate, and Caiaphas had 3*s.* 4*d.* or 4*s.* each, the CHRIST 2*s.*, Judas 1*s.* 6*d.*, and others in proportion to their importance, down to Pilate's son, 4*d.* It must be remembered that these amounts refer to one play only. The same characters, represented by different performers, would often appear in several pageants. The men who drew the pageant, and the minstrels who supplied the music, also required payment.

Another important item was refreshment for them and for the players. In 1490 the Coventry Smiths spent 2*s.* 2*d.* under this head at their first "reherse" in Easter week, and 2*s.* 4*d.* at the second in Whitsun week, while the expenses of the actual performance included 1*s.* 6*d.* for nine gallons of ale, "a rybbe of befe and j gose vj*d.*," and a second "rybbe of befe 3*d.*"

As a rule these expenses were cheerfully borne. It was recognized that the plays brought not only honour but profit to the town. Dugdale writes of the Coventry plays: "I have been told by some old people, who in their younger years were eye-witnesses of these Pageants so acted, that the yearly confluence of people to see that show was extraordinary great, and yeilded no small advantage to this City."[1] Additional attractions were provided by the songs and music of the minstrels who, as mentioned above, were hired for the occasion. In the Digby *Magdalene* a ship is brought in "with a mery song." Two songs have been preserved in the Coventry Shearmen's play: that of the shepherds with the refrain,

> "They sange terli terlow;
> So mereli the sheppards ther pipes can blow";

and that of the mothers of the Innocents,

> "By by, lully, lullay, thow
> littell tyne child."

The word "Daunce" in the margin of the Digby *S. Paul*, and a note to the Chester play of the Magi, "The boye and pigge when the kinges are gone"

[1] *Antiquities of Warwickshire* (1656), p. 116.

Plate II.

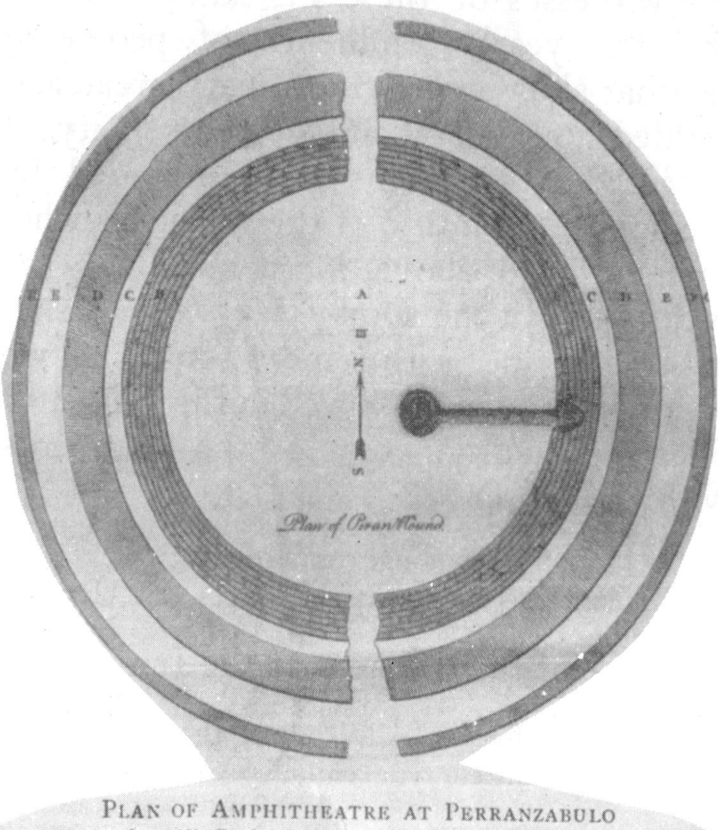

PLAN OF AMPHITHEATRE AT PERRANZABULO
(from W. Borlase's *Natural History of Cornwall*).

NOTE.—The pit in the centre, joined to the circumference by a trench, may have represented hell, but was more likely filled with water.

(See page 84 n.)

suggest that the performances might sometimes be interspersed with amusements of a more secular nature.

The plays were not necessarily given every year. The decision of this point and also the choice of plays to be performed rested with the municipal authorities. At York, an ordinance of 1476 decreed that a committee of four of the best players should be appointed in Lent to settle such matters, and to choose the players. Corpus Christi remained the normal season for the performance, partly, perhaps, because it was not far off the longest day. A passage already quoted (p. 68) shows that the *Ludus Coventriae* began at six o'clock. A York proclamation of 1378 ordered that the plays should begin at half-past four, and follow one another without tarrying; yet even with such precautions a single day was not always long enough for the performance. In 1456 Queen Margaret was at Coventry and saw "alle the pagentes pleyde save domesday, which might not be pleyde for lak of day." At Chester, as shown by the quotation from Archdeacon Rogers,[1] they were divided into three sets, which were played respectively on the Monday, Tuesday, and Wednesday in Whitsun week. The twenty-ninth pageant of the *Ludus Coventriae* is prefaced by an announcement that "we intendyn to procede the matere that we lefte the last yere." The prologue to the Digby *Massacre of the Innocents* suggests that it formed part of a series of which one was performed each year on S. Anne's Day.

The prologue to the *Ludus Coventriae* quoted above indicates that when a cycle was to be performed in a town the inhabitants of surrounding villages would be summoned to it. Otherwise the villages and smaller towns would depend for entertainment of this kind on isolated performances organized by the parish priest, or contributed by the occasional

[1] Above, pp. 79–81.

visits of professional players or of craftsmen from neighbouring towns, who were as willing to impress a rustic audience as to perform before the king.[1]

When Chaucer's wife of Bath enumerates "processiouns" and "pleyes of myracles" among her diversions, she is only giving evidence of a taste which she shared with all mediaeval England. The Lollard preacher might inveigh against the wickedness of turning God's mighty works into a means of amusement. The love of imitation and of spectacle was too deeply rooted for him to cut it out; how deeply the art and literature and common speech of the time bear witness.

Like many other mediaeval usages, however, the miracle plays fell victims to the religious upheavals of the sixteenth century. Puritan views began to gain ground; and the plays were suspect as savouring too much of "ceremonial

[1] Richard III saw the Coventry guild plays in 1484, and Henry VII in 1492.

religion." In 1548 the York cycle was shorn of the episodes representing the Death, Assumption, and Coronation of the Blessed Virgin. The reign of Mary brought a revival, but under Elizabeth reforming prelates forbade or discouraged the plays.

The growth of the secular drama (see chap. vi) also helped to bring about their downfall, which may be reckoned as completed by the end of the century, though isolated performances under James I are recorded. At Kendal in Westmorland they survived till 1612; a Passion Play was given at Ely House before the Spanish Ambassador, Gondomar, at some unknown date between 1613 and 1622; and in 1700 the Cornish plays were said to have been acted "in the memory of some not long since deceased."

Plate 12.

Photo] [*E. Trembath, St. Just.*

AMPHITHEATRE AT ST. JUST.

(See page 84 n.)

CHAPTER V

The Mediaeval Morals

THE remaining variety of mediaeval religious drama is known in modern English literature as the morality. This word, like "mystery," is borrowed from the French, and has no contemporary English authority. While the miracles endeavoured to instruct the spectators and stimulate their devotion by a reproduction of actual events as they happened,[1] the moral play, or moral, as it was called in England, supplemented them by applying the teachings of religion to the individual Christian

[1] In the mind of the mediaeval spectator this description would apply as well to the legends of the saints as to the events of the Gospel story.

by means of allegorical representations setting forth the perils and temptations which beset his soul. As the miracle play grew out of the liturgy, so the moral may be said to be a dramatic development of the sermon. Great preachers like S. Bernard made striking use of allegory and dialogue, but the process by which these methods of instruction grew into actual plays is obscure. Doubtless the mediaeval love of formal disputations had something to do with it. The popular dialogues called *débats* have already been mentioned.[1] The idea of a conflict between virtues and vices has been traced back to the *Psychomachia* of Prudentius, a Spaniard (born 348). This is a Latin poem describing a battle between the powers of good and evil, in which the several virtues engage in single combat with their corresponding vices after the manner of the heroes in Homer.

[1] P. 7.

We can also trace in the morals the influence of the grim mediaeval fantasy of the "Dance of Death," in which the King of Terrors lays his hand impartially on pope and peasant, on noble and beggar. A suggestion of this is found in the *Ludus Coventriae* when Death appears in person to strike down Herod. The same cycle introduces several allegorical characters. But, on the whole, the morals owe but little to the miracles. They may most probably be explained as an independent development of sermon and allegorical dialogue into dramatic form, intentionally fostered by the clergy as a vehicle of edification.

The one clear point of contact between the two kinds of play is the devil. As ruler of the powers of evil he naturally takes a leading part in the morals, which have for their subject the assault of those powers upon humanity. In the great miracle cycles the Evil One is by no means a comic character. His part in

Plate 13.

WOODEN MASK.
Worn by devil in Sixteenth-century German Play.

such incidents as the fall of the angels and the temptation of Eve is treated with the solemnity befitting a principal agent in the great drama. It was the minor devils who had early become comic favourites as they ran about among the spectators or dragged off souls to hell. We have seen how the Wakefield dramatist and his successors fastened on this vein of diabolic humour, and worked it up into one of the most popular features of the fifteenth century drama. Its extension to the moral plays was assisted by the personification of the Seven Deadly Sins as seven devils. The earliest moral of which we find any mention in England is the Pater Noster play which was performed by a "Guild of the LORD's Prayer" at York in 1378. There is evidence of plays on the same subject at Lincoln and at Beverley, where, in 1469, the LORD's Prayer was performed by the trade guilds in eight pageants. The seven petitions of the prayer were personified as Virtues, and in seven pageants each successively met and overcame one of the Deadly Sins, while the eighth pageant, either as prologue or epilogue, summed up the whole.

The Creed play acted every ten years by the York Guild of Corpus Christi, the earliest known performance being in 1446, may have been something of the same kind. Not a word of either of these has survived, though the York Pater Noster was performed as late as 1572. The earliest extant English moral is the fragmentary *Pride of Life* dating from the end of the fourteenth or beginning of the fifteenth century. Its hero, called *Rex Vivus*, the "King of Life," represents humanity. Confident in his knights Health and Strength, and in his messenger Mirth, he has the world at will. Disregarding the warnings of his queen and mocking at those of his bishop, whom he calls "byssop babler," he defies all enemies, even Death himself. Here the fragment breaks off, but we gather from the prologue that he was to be overthrown by Death, and his soul only saved by the prayers of our Lady.

The little play is brightly written with a good deal of humour, and the characters are not mere abstractions, but lifelike human beings. The earliest complete moral play, the *Castell of Perseverance*, which dates from about 1425, is much more typical of the class. It is dull and tedious, and its characters are little more than mouthpieces for the expression of various qualities. In leisurely mediaeval fashion it sets out in an elaborate allegory the fortunes of *Humanum Genus*, "Mankind," from the day of his birth until the final judgement is pronounced on his soul. The central episode, from which the play takes its name, is the siege of the Castle of Perseverance, "strenger thanne any in Fraunce," in which Mankind has taken refuge. The World, the Flesh, the Devil, and the Deadly Sins attack it, and are beaten off by the virtues. But in his old age Mankind gives himself up to Avarice. After his death the favourite dispute of Mercy and Peace against Righteousness and Truth concludes with the redemption of his soul from hell.

The Macro MS., in which it is preserved, contains a sketch of the stage arrangements together with invaluable indications of the manner in which the morals of this period were represented. A prologue announces the performance for "this day seuenenyt [sevennight]. . . . At . . . on the grene," and urges the populace to haste thither, and not to be late; thus indicating that it was acted in some central place to which the inhabitants of the surrounding towns and villages were summoned. The actual scene of performance was a circular *platea* or "place," surrounded, if practicable, by a moat full of water, and by five scaffolds on which the Deity, the Flesh, the World, the Devil, and Avarice were respectively stationed. In the middle of the place stood the castle containing a bed under which the soul was to be hid until Mankind's death gave him his cue to appear. The stage directions show how the actors moved about the "place" to the various scaffolds as occasion required, or mounted upon them.. The siege of the castle gave opportunity for a spectacular effect as the forces of evil advanced to the assault with banners and clarions, their leader, the Devil, having pipes filled with burning gunpowder attached to various parts of his person.

A play which has several points in common with the *Castell of Perseverance* is the Digby *Mary Magdalene*, which presents an interesting combination of the moral and miracle forms. It tells the story of the saint's life in much detail, showing her fall into sin, repentance, and anointing of our LORD's feet in the house of Simon the Leper. Then follow the stories of the raising of Lazarus, and the

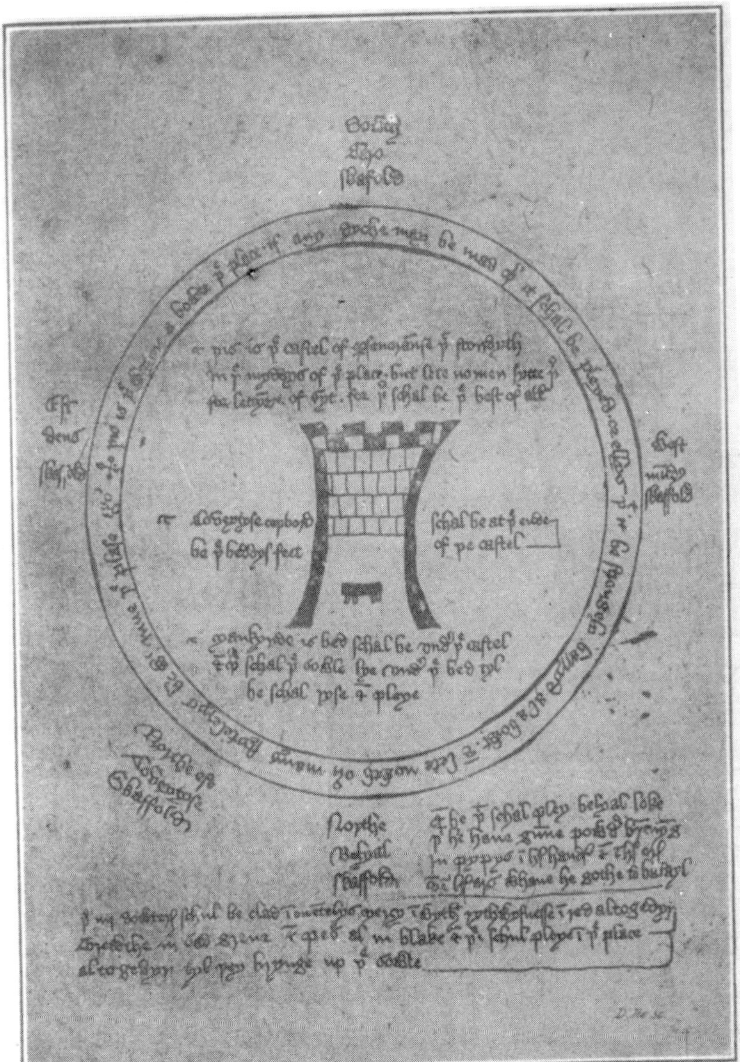

FIFTEENTH-CENTURY SKETCH GIVING DIRECTIONS FOR STAGING "THE CASTELL OF PERSEVERANCE."

Resurrection, the adventures of Mary Magdalene in the task of converting the King of Marseilles, and finally her life as a solitary in the wilderness and her death. Into the early part of this story are introduced the World, the Flesh, and the Devil plotting with the Deadly Sins against Mary, just as they plot against Mankind in the regular moral play. Lechery takes her to a tavern where she meets Curiosity, a swaggering dandy, who makes love to her. The devil scenes in this play referred to above[1] show how this popular feature of the stage was common to both kinds of play.

Other examples of the moral in its uncorrupted form are *Everyman* and *Wisdom*. The Dutch *Elckerlijk*, printed 1495, corresponds so closely to *Everyman* that one must be copied from the other, though the point of precedence between them is disputed. The subject, as is well known, is the approach of death, upon which the

[1] P. 74.

hero finds that Friendship, Kindred, and Wealth fail him, and only his Good Deeds remain. *Wisdom*, a play of about 1450, is also known as *Mind, Will, and Understanding*, from the three parts of the soul, who are seduced by Lucifer and converted by the Divine Wisdom. The Soul at first appears as "a mayde in a wyght clothe of golde," but after her fall "in the most horrybull wyse, fowlere than a fende" [fiend], with devils running in and out under her mantle.

From these examples it will be seen that the essential qualities of the moral were such as to preclude its development to any great extent as a species of religious drama. It was restricted to two or three plots, and these offered little scope for variety of incident or mode of treatment. The direction in which it did in fact advance is shown by the play of *Mankind*, written about 1475. In outline this play resembles those already described. The devils, under specious disguises, tempt

Plate 15.

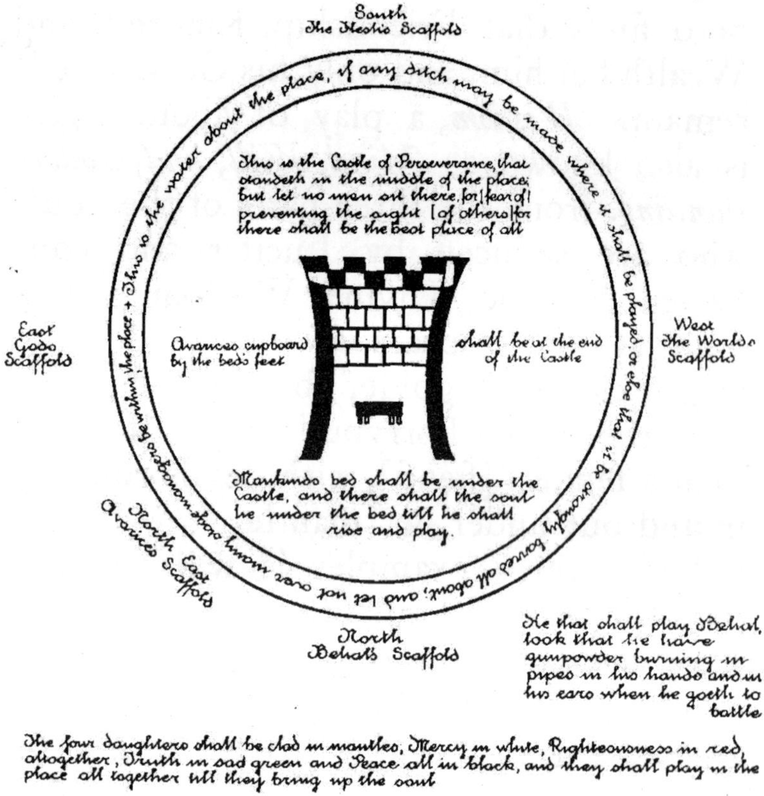

REPRODUCTION OF PLATE 14, WITH DIRECTIONS IN MODERN ENGLISH.

Mankind into evil courses till at last he repents, has recourse to Mercy and is forgiven. But the manner in which the theme is treated is altogether new. An atmosphere of broad, low comedy pervades the play, emanating from the devils, who are the centre of attraction. There is genuine humour in such scenes as those in which Tutivillus, their chief, spoils Mankind's digging by putting a board in the earth, or sends his satellites off on a freebooting expedition from which they return in various ridiculous plights. One feels that the author's interest and sympathy are with them, and not with the powers of good who for convention's sake win a formal victory. There are passages which clearly show that it was intended to be performed in the courtyard of an inn by a strolling company of professional actors. At the moment when the great devil is about to appear for the first time the actors announce their intention of making a collection, and that the spectators must be generous, "Ellys ther xall no man hym se." For—

> "He louyth [loveth] no grotis, nor pens or to-pens :
> Gyf us rede reyallys, if ye wyll se hys abhomynabull presens."

But, as "red royals"[1] may not be plentiful among the audience, another character thoughtfully adds, "Ye that mow not pay ye ton [may not pay the one], pay the tother."

We can now realize how the change of tone that has been noted was induced. The performers were no longer inspired by the desire to edify or to stimulate devotion, or even to do honour to their guild or their town. They were professionals earning their daily bread, and "we, that live to please, must please to live." If, as is probable enough, audiences could easily be sated with scholastic theology about the parts of the soul, as in *Wisdom*, or with the prolix disputa-

[1] Gold coins of the value of ten shillings.

tions of the *Castell of Perseverance*, they must be tempted with more attractive fare. The form of the moral must be retained, for it had not yet occurred to any one to write plays on other than religious subjects; but it must be made the vehicle for the coarse jests and buffoonery likely to draw the pennies and twopences from the pockets of the crowd who would assemble in winter[1] at an inn.

A somewhat similar tendency appears in *The Worlde and the Chylde*, which, though printed in 1522, belongs in spirit, and possibly in composition, to the preceding generation. The representative of humanity passes through various stages of life and is won over alternately by the World, by Conscience, by Folly, and by Perseverance. The play is free from the coarse vulgarity of *Mankind*, but the dramatic element in it preponderates over

[1] Several allusions show that this was the season of the performance.

Plate 16.

CHARACTERS IN "HYCKESCORNER"
(from Wynkyn de Worde's edition).

the didactic. The author's primary object is to relate what happens rather than to draw a lesson from it, and he carries out his purpose in a lively spirit of realism which foreshadows the later comedies of town life.

The same spirit appears in *Hyckescorner*, a moral of about the same date, which is notable for omitting altogether the representative of the human race who had hitherto served as the subject and prize of the conflict between good and evil. It has six characters—three virtues, who are still the conventional abstractions of the earlier period, and the three opposing vices in whom all the interest of the play is concentrated. In spite of their names[1] they are by no means mere abstractions, but very lifelike ruffians and swindlers whose boasts of their exploits convey an amusing description of the low life of the period.

[1] Hick the Scorner (or scoffer), Free Will, and Imagination.

It will be seen, therefore, that the moral as a form of drama, inspired by purely religious motives, enjoyed a considerably shorter career than the miracle. No trace of it is found before 1378, at which time the miracle cycles had been in existence some fifty years, and they had another century of chequered existence to run when, at the close of the fifteenth century, the strictly religious moral was wellnigh played out. Yet its influence on the future development of the drama can scarcely be overstated. The slow-moving cycle of twenty or thirty plays, whose performance occupied at least a long summer's day, was well suited to leisurely mediaeval habits, but could in no case have survived for long in a busier age.

Isolated miracle plays existed, it is true, unconnected with any cycle ; but it was left to the moral to reveal the full possibilities of the short self-contained play, suited for an afternoon's or evening's entertainment. Thus, while the *Castell of Perseverance*, the typical early moral, consists of nearly 4,000 lines, those which date from the end of the fifteenth century have only about 1,000 each; and with their short list of characters[1] exactly fit the capabilities of the little bands of travelling performers who, during that century, make their appearance among the minstrels and other entertainers, and were destined eventually to displace the craftsmen, as these had displaced the clergy, from the control and interpretation of the drama. They performed not only on the village green and at the inn, but also in the halls of the great. And everywhere alike their primary object was not to edify or to instruct, but to amuse. The effect in giving prominence to the comic possibilities of the moral has already been mentioned. And

[1] The parts are often so arranged as to be easily divided among four or six performers. This doubling of parts was probably facilitated by the use of masks.

it is clear that these possibilities lay in the hands of the evil qualities, since it was in character that they should revel with song and dance, play mischievous pranks, and mock the virtuous personages who in return could only instruct and exhort—a comparatively dull task. For this reason the bad qualities are found continually increasing in interest and importance. And the chief among them, distinguished as *the* "Vice" becomes the favourite and most prominent character in each play. Originally merely a personified Deadly Sin, whose business it was to lead the intrigue, he soon became a human character, the process being facilitated by his assuming various personalities—gallant, rogue, or ecclesiastic, as the plot might require. It was his function to keep the audience amused, and his original character of agent of evil was soon swallowed up in that of general mischief-maker, and eventually of jester, in which character he is the subject of frequent reference in sixteenth-century literature. Before this transformation was complete the moral itself had lost its purely religious tone and passed into the later stages of its history, which will be considered in the next chapter.

CHAPTER VI

Morals, Interludes, and the Elizabethan Drama

THE sixteenth century is the period of the birth and rise into greatness of the English secular drama. In the theatre, as in other paths, such as provision for the poor, and education, it has been the Church's lot to show the way, and then to retire, not always with the best grace, when secular agencies have learnt to follow it.

Any attempt to trace the dramatic history of the century would be quite outside the scope of this book. We can only note shortly the final stages of the development of the moral into a purely secular type of play, and the complete supersession of the religious by the secular drama, which took place before the close of the Tudor Period.

We have seen that the most common type of moral was that in which representatives of good and evil contended for the mastery over the human soul. In an age of many controversies, religious, political, and scholastic, the possibilities of this form of art were not likely to escape notice. With the political plays in which such characters as Liberty, Justice, Oppression, and Flattery vie with one another for influence with "Respublica" or "Albion" this book has nothing to do. More closely akin to the religious morals are those which show some typical representative of youth wavering between Idleness and Diligence, Ignorance and Instruction, and the like. These plays, like the ethical morals of the same period, teach that to follow Ignorance and Sensuality, instead of Learning and Reason, is folly, and brings evil consequences; but they have no spiritual motive, and do not concern themselves with the question of sin. Such topics would probably be more congenial to learned and courtly audiences than the less academic and more popular plays in which religious, and especially Protestant controversialists, seized on the form of the moral as a means of propagating their doctrines. That there is no subtlety about such a work as *New Custome* will appear from its list of characters, which includes, "Perverse Doctrine, an old popishe Priest," "Ignoraunce, an other but elder," "Light of the Gospel, a Minister."

The protagonist of this school was John Bale (1495–1563), an ex-Carmelite who became Bishop of Ossory in 1552. His *Three Lawes* is a violent and foul-mouthed attack on "popery"; the nature of which will be gathered from the direction that Sodomy is to be arrayed like a monk, False Doctrine like a popish doctor, and Hypocrisy like a grey friar.

In *Kynge Johan*, "Bilious Bale" strikes out a new line by choosing a subject from English history and casting it in the form of a moral. Its theme is King John's heroic defiance of Usurped Power, Private Wealth, and Sedition, who afterwards assume individuality as the pope, a cardinal, and Archbishop Stephen Langton. "Pristes channons and monkes, which do but fyll ther bely," are oppressing and impoverishing the country with "yowr pardons, yowr bulles, yowr purgatory pycke-purse, yowr lent fastes, yowr schryftes." Sedition brings in foreign enemies "with sheppes full of gonepowder," "with this Loller here to fyght," i.e. King John, who stands firm for the open Bible, and "as a faythfull Moyses Withstode proude Pharao," but in vain

"Tyll that duke Josue, whych was our late Kynge Henrye
Clerely brought us in to the lande of mylke and honye."

Dissimulation, a monk comes in singing, "Wassayle, wassayle out of the mylke payle," and, representing himself as Devotion, "as gentle a worm as ever ye see," poisons the king at the cost of sharing the draught himself, which gives occasion for a satirical dying speech :

"I do not doubte it but I shall be a saynt.
Provyde a gyldar myne image for to paynt.
I dye for the Churche with Thomas of Canterberye.
Ye shall fast my vigyll and upon my daye be merye.
No doubt but I shall do myracles in a whyle,
And therefore lete me be shryned in the north yle."

It is interesting to observe that *Kynge Johan* is the first extant English historical play,[1] and, as such, its development from the controversial moral is worth noticing, though it exercised but little influence on later plays on the same subject.

[1] No doubt Bale's lost play *De imposturis Thomae Becketi* was another of the same kind.

Nevertheless Bale's view of the character of John was commonly accepted until the greater dramatic possibilities of the fate of Arthur were discovered, and the legend of the Wicked Uncle superseded the legend of the Protestant Hero.

The Tudor sovereigns were not likely to overlook the value of the drama as a weapon of controversy, or the desirability of keeping it under their own control. A statute of 1543 (34–35 Hen. VIII, c. 1) expressly permits the performance of plays "for the rebuking and reproching of vices, and the setting foorth of vertue," so long as their teaching is not "contrarye to the doctryne set foorthe by the King's Majestie." In 1559, however, Elizabeth found it advisable to prohibit all plays dealing with debateable matters of religion or politics; it is probable that this policy contributed to the complete secularization of the stage. Once the drama had established its right to exist for the purpose of enter-

SCENE FROM "HYCKESCORNER"
(from title-page of an early edition.) (See page 115.)

tainment apart from edification, it was safer for all concerned that it should confine itself thereto. And the Puritan prejudice against the public representation of sacred subjects no doubt assisted in the process.

In the preceding chapter reference was made to the appearance of professional players, whose performances in banqueting-halls and private houses brought about a modification in the form of the moral. What was required on such occasions was not a long didactic exposition, but a short dramatic entertainment. In this way there was evolved a kind of play which is commonly and conveniently known as the interlude,[1] though for a long time this term was applied to all plays of the moral form, whether religious in purpose or not. The interlude, in this sense,

[1] The word probably means a *Ludus* played between two or more performers, not, as often supposed, in the intervals of something else. See *Med. Stage* ii. 183.

represents the last stage in the history of the moral. It has no religious, ethical, or controversial purpose, but is designed merely to amuse, though its chief comedian is still called the Vice, and abstractions are often mixed with real people among its characters.

Now, as at an earlier period, features were sometimes borrowed from the miracle drama. *King Daryus* (1565), which is described as "A Pretie new Enterlude both pithie and plesaunt," is really a piece of Protestant controversy with a Vice, Iniquity, who boasts of his father the Pope. But Lewis Wager's *Marie Magdalene* (1566–67) is a genuine combination of the two types and more devotional in tone than most of its contemporaries. The heroine enters grumbling that her garments are made by "the most bungarliest tailers in this countrie." Infidelity the Vice plans her downfall, and also plots with Simon the Pharisee and Malicious Judgment against our LORD. The play ends with the scene in Simon's house.

It is worth remarking that on Mary's forgiveness the devils "without the doore" are heard to "roare terribly." When reading the fifteenth-century play on this subject we must imagine a circular "place" with Hell among various other localities, all within sight of the spectators the whole time. Now we have to do with a single stage, at the end of a banqueting-hall or the like, representing, if necessary, various places in turn, with entrances and exits made through a fixed door, beyond which the characters are invisible to the spectators. The woodcut on the title-page of *The Three Lordes and Three Ladies of London* apparently represents the performance of such an interlude, the audience being shown seated on a dais.

Though the representation of anything like a miracle cycle under such conditions was out of the question, individual

Plate 18.

THE PERFORMANCE OF AN INTERLUDE
(from *The Three Lordes and Three Ladies of London*, 1590).
(See page 129.)

miracle plays were sometimes performed in halls and houses even in the fifteenth century; and the fact that some sixteenth-century interludes followed the miracles in drawing on Holy Scripture for their plots contributed to the transition from the moral, in which the characters are abstract qualities, to the drama of real life. Two of Bale's plays, *Johan Baptystes Preachynge*, and *The Temptacyon of Our Lorde*, are pure miracles with no admixture of the moral element. They are also less controversial than his other extant works, though in the *Temptacyon* the baffled fiend cannot resist the remark, "Thy vycar at Rome, I thynke, wyll be my frynde [friend]."

Finally in *Jacob and Esau* (licensed 1557–58) we find the interlude definitely growing into the play. It is styled "A newe mery and wittie Comedie or Enterlude," and tells its story in romantic fashion by means of skilfully-drawn characters.

We are now on the threshold of the Elizabethan drama. To that mighty edifice the religious drama may claim to have been a principal contributor through the development of the moral into a comedy of contemporary life and manners.[1] In the last decades of the century we find such elaborate comedies as *The Three Ladies of London* (1584), and *The Three Lordes and Three Ladies of London* (1590), still following the morals in calling their characters Love, Lucre, Dissimulation, Pride, and the like.

Still more curious is *The Conflict of Conscience* (1581), which deals with a story taken from real life, but turns it into a moral by substituting Philologus, Theo-

[1] In *The Evolution of the English Drama up to Shakespeare* (Berlin, 1912), published after these pages were written, Dr. C. Wallace contends that the influence of court entertainments, masques, and interludes, independent of the religious plays, was a more important factor in the development of the drama than has hitherto been supposed.

logus, and so on, for the names of the persons concerned. In some of the plays of Shakespeare's greatest contemporaries we find stray survivals of odds and ends from the religious drama. Such a play as Peele's *David and Bethsabe* owes nothing but its plot to Holy Scripture. The comic devil in Greene's *Frier Bacon and Frier Bongay* is merely a reminiscence of a popular feature of the old plays. In *The Devil is an Ass* Jonson introduces a devil and a Vice, in the same spirit of irony in which, in *The Staple of News*, he makes a character say, "My husband . . . was wont to say there was no play without a fool and a devil in 't; he was for the devil still, God bless him! The devil for his money, would he say, I would fain see the devil . . . he would carry away the Vice on his back, quick to hell, in every play where he came, and reform abuses."

Greene's *Looking Glass for London* employs some of the features of the religious drama in a more serious spirit; and in *Faustus* Marlowe deliberately reverts to the now archaic religious moral by bringing in a Good and a Bad Angel and a Procession of Deadly Sins. The central idea of Dekker's *Old Fortunatus*, the conflict between Virtue and Fortune for the allegiance of mankind, is also that of *The Contention between Liberalitie and Prodigalitie*, an ethical moral acted before Elizabeth in 1601.

By this time the form of the moral play was merely a survival from an extinct order of things. All that was living and effective in the religious plays had been absorbed into the secular theatre. Bereft of its best elements the purely religious drama flickered down to the brainless pantomime of puppet-shows and village mummings, to be described in the next chapter.

Hitherto we have been considering principally the development of the moral into the comedy. The fact that the direct influence of the miracles on the Elizabethan drama is less marked is, no doubt, due to the stereotyped form of the great cycles which had reached the highest point of development of which they were capable in the fifteenth century. Their influence may, however, be discerned in the long, rambling chronicle plays which preceded the histories of Shakespeare. On the other hand, the direct debt of English tragedy to the religious drama is comparatively small. The early tragic writers drew their inspiration from classical sources and especially from Seneca, rather than from the morals or the miracles. The reason for this distinction is not far to seek. Christian drama must necessarily approximate to the form of comedy rather than of tragedy. Its dramatic reversal of fortune lies, not in the fall from prosperity to adversity, which, as Aristotle teaches, is the essence of tragedy, but in triumph after apparent defeat, the joy of Easter (germ of all Christian drama) after Good Friday, the victory of the martyr over death, the overthrow of the apparently victorious powers of evil. The miracle cycles themselves might well be called Divine Comedies, dealing as they do with the age-long struggle and final triumph of redeemed humanity. It was a true instinct which led Hrotsvitha, the first Christian dramatist, to take a writer of comedy as her model; and for the same reason the persistent tendency to introduce the comic element was natural and appropriate.

We may, therefore, conclude that Elizabethan and later English comedy is the direct outcome of the religious drama, mainly by way of the development of the moral. Other influences, it is true, contributed to it, such as the revived study of the classics. With these we are not now concerned. It is more germane to our purpose to note the indications of its religious ancestry which have permanently survived in English drama. The most important of these is its entire freedom from the supposed obligation to observe the "unities," which binds any drama that prides itself on following classical models. Here we may detect the influence of the miracle cycles with their continual changes of subject and scene, and their mingling of the comic with the serious element. The fact that no women appeared on the English professional stage till after the Restoration may be in part referred to its descent from the liturgical drama which was acted by priests and chanters. The custom of giving the characters of a play names descriptive of their dispositions or occupations arose from the personified qualities of the morals, was carried to excess by Jonson, continued by the Restoration dramatists, with their Brisks and Maskwells, and survived well into the nineteenth century.

We have now followed the religious

drama in England to the close of its separate existence. Such straggling remnants as survived the sixteenth century will be considered in the next chapter, and that which follows will deal with the revival of the drama as a religious art after the lapse of three hundred years.

CHAPTER VII

Some Results of Puritanism

WHEN the Bible story ceased to provide subjects for living actors it was taken over by the puppet-shows or "motions," which first became popular in the sixteenth century. These are thought to have originated in the representations of sacred scenes in churches by groups of small figures, the Christmas "crib" being the standing example. There is evidence that representations of the Resurrection by means of moving figures were sometimes given in church. But by the end of the sixteenth century exhibitions of this sort were confined to professional showmen whose repertory included secular as well as sacred subjects. The puppet-showman in Jonson's *Bartholomew Fair* can represent Hero and Leander, and Gunpowder Plot, as well as Bible stories. Such performances can scarcely be called religious drama, but they deserve mention as the only scriptural plays which survived in England through the seventeenth century. Puppet-shows of the Creation, the Flood, and Dives and Lazarus are recorded in the reign of Anne. One play-bill announces "Noah and his family coming out of the ark, with all the beasts two by two, and all the fowls of the air seen in a prospect sitting upon trees; likewise over the ark is seen the sun rising in a glorious manner: moreover, a multitude of angels will be seen in a double rank." The nature of these exhibitions may also be inferred from an account given in No. 16 of *The Tatler*, May 17, 1709, which mentions that "*Punch* and his wife were introduced dancing in the ark."[1] As late as 1818

[1] The Italian "Punchinello" first appears in England about 1666. There is no foundation for the belief that the name "Punch and Judy" is derived from *Pontius cum Judaeis*. This popular

"PULL DEVIL, PULL BAKER."
Acted by puppets at Bartholomew Fair.
(From H. Morley's *Memoirs of Bartholomew Fair.*)

William Hone saw a "Gallantee" show[1] of the Prodigal Son, the Flood, and *Pull Devil, Pull Baker*, "or the just judgment upon a baker who sold short of weight, and was carried to hell in his own basket." It is interesting to know that in 1888 puppets were employed in Paris as the medium for representing one of the earliest of Christian dramas, the *Abraham* of Hrotsvitha.[2]

While the scriptural drama in England thus dwindled to the dimensions of a puppet-show, the saints' plays survived only in the debased form of village mummings, the evolution of which can be traced back to pre-Christian times, and

show is only connected with the religious drama as being the sole survivor in England of the puppet plays.

[1] Defined in the *New English Dictionary* as "a shadow pantomime produced by throwing shadows of miniature figures on a wall or screen."

[2] Lemercier de Neuville, *Historie des Marionettes*, Paris, 1892, p. 146.

eventually to the ceremonial dance in which students of folk-lore have found the primal origin of all drama[1] and most religion. Among the most important of these ceremonies was that which symbolized winter and spring, the death and resurrection of the year. Out of this grew a folk-drama, the central incident of which was the slaying and revival of one of the characters. The popularity of S. George as the national champion of mediaeval England caused his pageant, or play, to be grafted into this. The result was a village play, which shows traces also of another ancient rite, the

[1] See Courthope, *History of English Poetry*, i. 401, for the course taken by English and ancient Greek drama respectively in their development from religious ceremonial. The drama of India and other countries is traced to its origin in the religious dance in A. W. Ward's article "Drama," in the *Encyclopaedia Britannica*; in Persia an elaborate "Passion Play" has sprung out of the annual ceremony of lamentation for the tragic fate of Ali, the son-in-law of Mohammed, and his house.

sword-dance. The existing texts, handed down by oral tradition, prove it to have been a saint's play only in name. Its roots are deep in primitive religion. As a popular rustic festivity it survived the Reformation, endured through the Hanoverian period, when its hero sometimes became "King," or "Prince" George, and still exists in some parts of England at the present time.

The reader will have gathered that the influence of the sixteenth century upon the purely religious drama was, for the most part, of a destructive character. One original contribution, however, stands to its credit, and was destined to possess considerable vitality, namely, the burning of the pope in effigy. This ceremony has been traced back to 1570, when it took placed on Elizabeth's Accession Day, November 17th, a date which led to its being assimilated to the winter bonfire of primitive folk-religion. At the end of the seventeenth century, a period favourable to anti-papal demonstrations, the day was observed in London by a procession "in honour of the established religion, and in ridicule of the Pope," whose effigy, holding the keys "of a place he is never likely to get into," and attended by his "right trusty and well-beloved cousin" the devil, was burned at Temple Bar. In Anne's reign the Pretender was added to the group. *The Coronation of Elizabeth*, a play acted at Bartholomew Fair in 1680, which would otherwise be worthless, provides an indication of the sentiments of the time. The pope, assisted by the devil "in the shape of a Jesuit," plots Elizabeth's death, for "Blood and Murthers are Rome's chiefest glories." But, after seeing a vision of "Hell full of Devils, Popes, and Cardinals," he is burned by the queen's loyal subjects. In modern times this festival, transferred to the anniversary of Gunpowder Plot, retains few traces either of its former glories or of its anti-papal origin.

It is something of a paradox that the greatest of Puritans, John Milton, should have produced in *Samson Agonistes* and *Comus* plays which, at any rate, approximate to the types respectively of miracle and moral. Like other great poets, he was attracted by the dramatic form.[1] But, though *Comus* was performed by amateurs at Ludlow Castle in 1634, these isolated experiments are not inconsistent with the fact that the effect of the period of Puritan domination, following as it did upon the complete secularization of the theatre, was to establish the belief that religion and the drama were not merely distinct, but antagonistic forces. This was an impression which the comedy of the Restoration was certainly not calculated to remove. And the commonplace and materialistic view of the eighteenth century is ironically

[1] He is said to have contemplated a *Christus Patiens* and other scriptural plays.

expressed in the words which Sheridan places in the mouth of Sneer in *The Critic*: "The theatre, in the proper hands, might certainly be made the school of morality; but now, I am sorry to say it, people seem to go there principally for their entertainment." Not only are no religious plays worthy the name found in England during the period under consideration in this chapter,[1] but those which English travellers witnessed on the Continent are described in a spirit of good-humoured contempt as relics of a superstition suited to the intelligence of foreigners, but long since outgrown by John Bull. Several descriptions in this tone of eighteenth and early nineteenth century plays are quoted by Hone, who also cites Thomas Moore's account of

[1] The *Sacred Dramas* of Hannah More (1782) are only an apparent exception to this statement, being designed merely for the moral instruction of the young, and not for representation.

the Parisian theatres from *The Fudge Family in Paris* (1818):

> "And doubtless, so fond they're of scriptural facts,
> They will soon get the Pentateuch up in five acts.
> Here Daniel in pantomime bids bold defiance
> To Nebuchadnezzar and all his stuff'd lions."

In spite of English disapproval the religious drama survived in the Roman Catholic parts of Europe, and to them we must look for its history in the seventeenth and eighteenth centuries and the greater part of the nineteenth. The Spanish dramatist Lope de Vega (1562–1635), besides his fifteen hundred plays, which included many in honour of the miracles of the saints, wrote some four hundred *autos Sacramentales*, or scenes to be performed in the open air during processions of the Blessed Sacrament. These exhibitions were forbidden in Spain in 1765.

The French dramatists of the seventeenth century also drew, though more sparingly, on sacred sources for their themes. Those of Corneille's tragedies *Polyeucte* (1643) and *Théodore* (1645) are taken from Christian martyrology; and Racine's *Esther* (1689) and *Athalie* (1691) still hold their place among the masterpieces of the French classical stage.

But for the purposes of a history of the religious drama the most notable of the Continental plays of this period is that founded at the Bavarian village of Ober Ammergau in 1634,[1] in fulfilment of a vow made in time of pestilence. It was excepted from the general suppression of religious plays in Bavaria at the end of the eighteenth and beginning of the nineteenth century; and in recent times its decennial performances have drawn many thousands of spectators from all parts of the world. The theatre holds four thousand persons, and about thirty

[1] There is evidence, however, of the existence of a "Passion Play" there in the Middle Ages.

Plate 20.

SCENE FROM OBER AMMERGAU PLAY IN THE SEVENTEENTH CENTURY.

Judas leaves the Last Supper. An Angel takes away his halo.

From *Ober Ammergau and its Passion Play*, by H. Deimer.

representations are given at each revival. The play represents the Gospel story from Palm Sunday to the Ascension, interspersed with choruses and illustrative tableaux from the Old Testament. It lasts from eight in the morning till five or six at night, with an interval of about two hours. There are a hundred and twenty-five speaking parts and nearly seven hundred performers in all. Since 1850 all traces of the comic and grotesque have been strictly eliminated, and the world-famous peasants play their parts in a spirit of simple reverence which is not inconsistent with histrionic genius, fine music, and beautiful stage-setting.

Though somewhat overshadowed by the reputation of Ober Ammergau, similar plays are cxtant at various places in Southern Germany and the Tyrol. Perhaps the most noteworthy is that performed at Erl, a village between Munich and Innsbruck. It is at least as

Plate 21.

[F. Bruckmann, A.G., Munich.

THE PASSION PLAY AT OBER AMMERGAU.

JESUS entering Jerusalem (from the Ober Ammergau Passion Play, 1910).

old as the Ober Ammergau play, which it is considered by competent judges to rival both in artistic merit and in the spirit of reverent devotion. The modern Passion Play, performed every few years at Selzach in Switzerland, is noteworthy as an offshoot from Ober Ammergau, in imitation of which it was founded at the end of the last century.

Besides the Passion Plays proper, a number of old French and German Nativity Plays, comparatively unknown to travellers owing to the season of their representation, survived until late in the nineteenth century, and in some places are still to be seen. In the Epiphany Plays which are still acted in the villages of Majorca the Sibyl retains her ancient place among the prophets. But the Magi themselves are quite overshadowed by the comic business. And the carrying off of Herod by the devil is regarded as the culmination of the

Plate 22.

Group from Erl Passion Play.

performance, the actual adoration being perfunctorily played to the backs of the retiring audience.

The quasi-dramatic processions which still survive at some places on the Continent must also be mentioned; especially the Procession of the Holy Blood at Bruges, which is held every year in May on the Monday after Holy Cross Day, and that which takes place at Furnes near Ostend on the last Sunday in each July. Groups representing scriptural episodes take part in these processions as they did in the mediaeval "ridings."[1] And at Furnes, scenes from the life of our Lord are drawn through the streets on scaffolds after the manner of the "pageants."

Besides the plays, which are acted primarily for religious purposes, travellers in Roman Catholic countries still occasionally light upon rude, but in spirit not

[1] Above, p. 54.

irreverent, representations of scriptural scenes by professional players.[1]

[1] See a description of such performances in the Black Forest, the Pyrenees, and at Mechlin in Baring Gould, *Germany, Present and Past* (1879), ii. 8–9 ; also a reference to a Passion Play performed by "a company of comedians" at Tarragona on Easter Eve, 1869, in *Notes and Queries*, fourth series, vi. 4. A Nativity Play is still acted by professionals at Naples every Christmas.

CHAPTER VIII

The Modern Revival

WE have seen in the preceding chapter the pitiful condition into which the religious drama fell in England after the Elizabethan period. The fortunes of the secular theatre during the same time may be briefly summarized. Its complete severance from religion under Elizabeth and James I was quickly followed by "the Reign of the Saints," one result of which was to implant in the English mind the conviction that the stage is in its nature an evil thing rather than a potential agent for good. This belief, which is still far from extinct, reacted on the secular drama. Its demoralizing effects are to be seen in the tone of the comedies in which the Restoration playwrights devoted themselves to reproducing the manners of the town under Charles II, comedies which can only be defended on the ground, taken by Charles Lamb, that "they are a world of themselves almost as much as fairyland," one "where no cold moral reigns," and "which has no reference whatever to the world that is." In the eighteenth century, English comedy was purged of its indecency and of a good deal of its wit, but it remained equally remote from life, concerning itself only with the artificial intrigues and conventional unrealities of the stage. This state of things continued for a great part of the nineteenth century, in spite of isolated attempts at restoring the drama, made by Browning, Tennyson, and others.

The honour of taking the first effective step towards bringing the theatre once more into relations with real life belongs to T. W. Robertson (1829–71).

Photo] [*Miss Caswall Smith.*

JOSEPH IN "THE DREAMER."

(See page 163.)

Though any detailed consideration of his work and that of his artistic descendants would be outside our scope, we must remember that by restoring the conception of the theatre as a place where serious questions can be treated in terms of art, by vindicating, that is, the right of the drama to stand on a level with other forms of art in this respect, they helped to make possible the revival of the religious drama.

Another factor was the romantic revival of which Sir Walter Scott was the first great leader. After many struggles and apparent defeats this movement, the counterpart of the Catholic revival in the Church, succeeded in convincing the expiring nineteenth century that the Middle Ages were not merely an orgy of superstitious brutality, and that a drab utilitarianism is not necessarily the last word of civilization. Among its results was the popularity in the early years of this century of the "Pageants" in which dramatic representations of Church history held a prominent place.

Another and less happy sign of the times is to be found in the pseudo-religious plays, which have enjoyed a considerable vogue. Their authors sought in vain to create a religious drama by flinging religious emotionalism on the stage in raw lumps instead of transmuting it through the medium of art.

That there was a genuine, if unconscious, demand for definitely religious drama was shown by the success of the fifteenth-century *Everyman* when revived in 1901. This demand has been met and stimulated by the revival of other old plays, and also by the creation of a new religious drama, which, while avoiding a merely archaic reproduction of the mediaeval form, endeavours to make the same appeal to the heart and conscience.

Among such plays may be mentioned *Bethlehem*, by Laurence Housman (1902),

Plate 24.

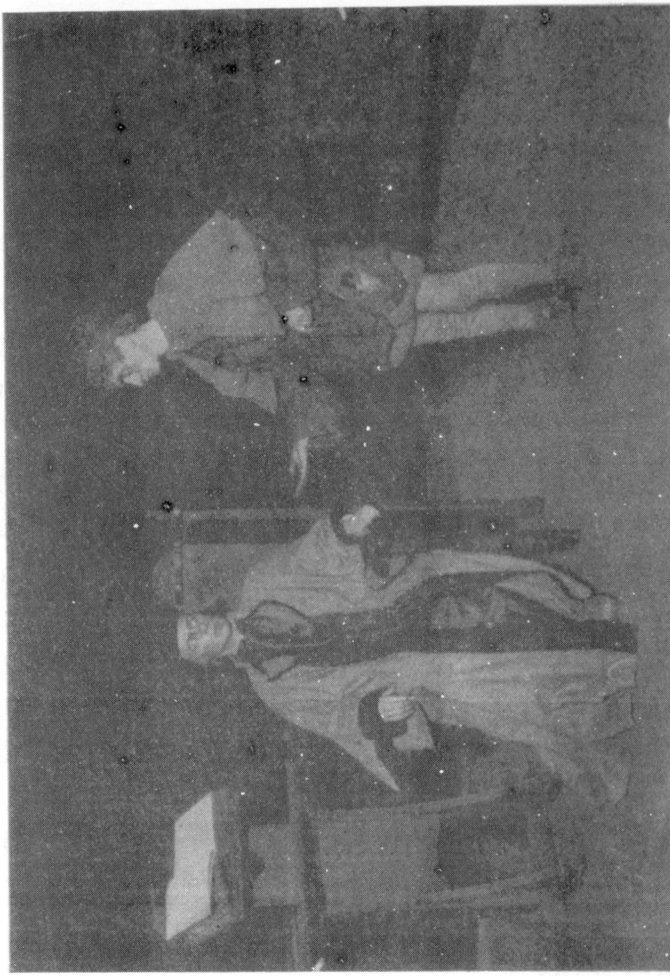

Photo] [London News Agency.

SCENE FROM "THE HOUR GLASS."

in which the story of the Nativity is retold in a spirit of reverent and delicate simplicity; *Eager Heart*, a Christmas allegory, by A. M. Buckton (1904); *The Hour Glass*, "a Morality," by W. B. Yeats (1904); *The Soul of the World*, "a Mystery Play of the Nativity and the Passion," by M. Dearmer (1911); and *The Dreamer*, by the same author (1912), a play setting forth the story of Joseph "first historically, and then symbolically as a type of the CHRIST to come." *Epiphany*, "a Twelfth Night Interlude," by J. G. Adderley (1912), is a play of modern life which applies its religious motive directly to social problems.

Some of these have been put on the stage by the Morality Play Society, which was founded in 1911 for the purpose of producing plays "which find their inspiration in an ideal motive," and thus of assisting the drama to escape from the degrading associations into which it has been forced by Puritanism, and to vindicate its right to treat religious and moral questions in a reverent and artistic spirit.

The widespread influence of this revival is shown by the village and other local plays, secular as well as religious, which in recent years have sprung up spontaneously in various parts of the country. From the Christmas crib many parishes have passed on to the "Bethlehem Tableaux," and from these to the Nativity or other sacred play. Special mention must be made of that performed every Innocents' Day in the Parish of Hambridge, Somerset. It is founded on the Towneley *Secunda Pastorum*,[1] but the whole of the dialogue is left to the inspiration of the moment, and is thus the natural outcome of the religious feeling of the peasant child-actors. For example, one shepherd will say, "They zongs of David about the King of Glory and such like: they promises we do hear to Temple, they doant zim to come to

[1] Above, p. 65.

Plate 25.

Photo] [The Daily Mirror.

THE HAMBRIDGE NATIVITY PLAY.

Discovery of the stolen lamb in Mak's cottage.

nothink do 'en, not yits know?" "No a doant," his fellow will reply, "but I zim as there be stirrings, George: and I wont say as they might not come." Or our Lady, picking up the Child, may remark to S. Joseph, "You say Mak be a bad fellow; so a be; but I reckon here be One as can make summat o' he."

All such evidence of the revival of the drama as a religious influence in the life of the people is welcome. But it is scarcely to be expected that under modern conditions plays directly religious in form and subject-matter can exercise the same power over the soul of the nation as in the Middle Ages. If the drama is to attain any such influence to-day it must be through the more widespread and popular appeal of the ordinary professional theatre, carried on primarily as a commercial undertaking. We have already seen how, of late years, the secular drama has begun to reassert its claim to a

Plate 26.

Photo] [London News Agency.

SCENE FROM "THE TRAVELLING MAN," BY LADY GREGORY.

foremost place among the arts. This movement is not confined to England. Foreign dramatists such as Maurice Maeterlinck with his "exquisite tragic symbolism," Henrik Ibsen (1828–1906) with his sombre genius, Björnsterne Björnson (1832–1910), Gerhart Hauptmann, and Herman Sudermann, may justly take their place among the first writers of the age. The revival of the national poetic drama of Ireland in the hands of such authors as Lady Gregory, J. M. Synge, and W. B. Yeats, bears witness to the same upward tendency. And in England we have writers whose plays, religious in motive and spirit, if not in form, bring all the resources of the dramatic art to bear on the social and economic questions which most nearly concern the nation at the present day.

In plays like *Candida*[1] (1898) and *John Bull's Other Island*[2] (1907), *Justice*[3] (1906)

[1] By George Bernard Shaw. [2] Ibid.
[3] By John Galsworthy.

and *The Silver Box*[1] (1910), *The Voysey Inheritance*[2] (1909) and *Chains*[3] (1911), the forces which lie in wait for contemporary Mankind are exposed and fought as surely and as sincerely as in any mediaeval play; and the spiritual conflict is interpreted in terms of dramatic art by some of the leading playwrights of our time.

It is true that authors of this school are by no means necessarily Churchmen or Christians. But their plays, nevertheless, constitute a strong moral and religious force. It is for the Church to complete the work by taking its part in this dramatic revival, and using it as an ally in the conflict with the powers of evil. The inevitable result of adopting the Puritan attitude is to drive the theatre into the arms of the enemy, and so to produce the very result we deplore. For

[1] By John Galsworthy.
[2] By Harley Granville Barker.
[3] By Elizabeth Baker.

good or evil a movement is in progress, the outcome of which must be that the drama will exercise a more powerful influence on the life and thought of the nation than it has possessed at any time since the sixteenth century. It is the task of the Church to breathe the spirit of Christianity into this movement, and so to enable the drama to occupy worthily its position as a religious art.

BIBLIOGRAPHY

THE following list of authorities is intended to assist the reader to verify the statements in the text, and to indicate the direction which further study in the subject may profitably take. Those who desire to go into the matter more thoroughly will find full and valuable bibliographies in the works marked *.

NOTE.—To save space in the footnotes works contained in this list are usually referred to by the author's name only ; the full titles and other particulars will be found below.

ABBREVIATIONS.—E.E.T.S., Early English Text Society. Sh. Soc., Shakespeare Society.

GENERAL BIBLIOGRAPHY FOR CHAPTERS I—VI

A. W. Ward—*History of English Dramatic Literature*, 1899; and art. "Drama" in *Encyclopaedia Britannica*, eleventh edition, 1910.

**The Cambridge History of English Literature.* Edited by A. W. Ward and A. R. Waller. Vol. v, 1910.

W. J. Courthope—*History of English Poetry*. Vol. i (1895), chap. x ; Vol. ii (1904), chap. xi.

*E. K. Chambers—*The Mediaeval Stage*, 1903.

C. M. Gayley—"An Historical View of English Comedy," in *Representative English Comedies*, 1903; and *Plays of our Forefathers*, 1907.

A. W. Pollard—*English Miracle Plays*. Fifth edition, 1909.

V. E. Albright—*The Shakesperian Stage*. (Columbia University Studies in English, 1909.)

*C. F. Tucker Brooke—*The Tudor Drama*, 1912.

J. M. Manly—*Specimens of the Pre-Shaksperean Drama*, 1897.

FOR CHAPTER I

Christus Patiens—Edited by J. G. Brambs, Lipsiae, 1885.

Hrotsvithae Opera—Edited by K. Strecker, Lipsiae, 1906.

C. Magnin—*Théatre de Hrotsvitha*. Paris, 1845.

The Harrowing of Hell—Edited by W. H. Hulme. E.E.T.S., 1907.

FOR CHAPTERS II, III, IV

An English Miscellany, 1901—Including "A Note on the Origin of the Liturgical Drama," by Pierce Butler; "A Note on Pageants and 'Scaffolds Hye,'" by J. J. Jusserand; "Some English Plays and Players, 1220–1548," by A. F. Leach.

W. H. Frere—*The Winchester Troper.* Henry Bradshaw Society, 1894.

J. J. Champollion-Figeac—*Hilarii Versus et Ludi.* Paris, 1838.

T. Wright—*Early Mysteries*, 1838.

C. Davidson—*Studies in the English Mystery Plays*, 1892. (Transactions of the Connecticut Academy, ix.)

S. B. Hemingway—*English Nativity Plays.* (Yale Studies in English, 1909.)

T. Sharp—*Dissertation on Pageants*, 1825.

EDITIONS OF PLAYS REFERRED TO IN CHAPTER IV

"The York Cycle"—Edited by L. T. Smith, 1885.

"The Chester Cycle"—Edited by T. Wright, Sh. Soc., two vols., 1843–47; Plays 1–13—Edited by H. Deiling, E.E.T.S., 1893.

"The Towneley Cycle"—Edited for the Surtees Society, 1836; edited by G. England and A. W. Pollard, E.E.T.S., 1897.

Ludus Coventriae—Edited by J. O. Halliwell, Sh. Soc., 1841.

"The Cornish Cycle"—Edited by E. Norris, 1841.

"The Coventry Guild Plays"—Edited by H. Craig, E.E.T.S., 1902.

"The Digby Plays"—Edited by F. J. Furnival, New Sh. Soc., 1882; E.E.T.S., 1896.

The Brome, Dublin, Croxton, and Newcastle Plays are in *Non-Cycle Mystery Plays*—Edited by O. Waterhouse, E.E.T.S., 1909.

Some episodes from the cycles and isolated plays may be found in Manly, Pollard, and other collections.

CHAPTER V

E. N. S. Thompson—*The English Moral Plays.* (Connecticut Academy of Arts and Sciences, 1910.)

L. W. Cushman—*The Devil and the Vice.* Halle, 1900.

EDITIONS OF THE PLAYS REFERRED TO IN CHAPTER V

The Pride of Life is in *Non-Cycle Mystery Plays* (above), *Mankind*, *Wisdom*, and *The Castell of Perseverance*, are edited, as *The Macro Plays*, by F. J. Furnivall and A. W. Pollard, E.E.T.S., 1904. *Mankind* is also in Manly, and "*Lost*" *Tudor Plays*, edited by J. S. Farmer, 1907.

Everyman, four sixteenth century editions; *Dodsley's Old Plays*, edited by W. C. Hazlitt, 1874–76, i; J. S. Farmer, *Anonymous Plays*, first series, 1905; and various other editions.

The Worlde and the Chylde, 1532; *Dodsley*, i. Manly; Farmer, *Anonymous Plays*, first series.

Hyckescorner, early sixteenth century editions, n.d.; *Dodsley*, i; Manly; Farmer, *Anonymous Plays*, first series.

All the above plays, except *The Pride of Life* and *Everyman*, are issued in *The Tudor Facsimile Texts*, edited by J. S. Farmer, 1907–09.

EDITIONS OF PLAYS REFERRED TO IN CHAPTER VI

New Custome, 1573; *Dodsley*, iii; Farmer, *Anonymous Plays*, third series, 1906; *Tudor Facsimile Texts*, 1908.

John Bale—*Dramatic Writings*, edited by J. S. Farmer, 1907. Besides the sixteenth century editions of single plays, *The Three Lawes*, and *The Temptacyon of Our Lorde* are in *Tudor Facsimile Texts*, 1908–09; *Kynge Johan*, edited by J. P. Collier, Camden Society, 1838; Manly.

King Daryus, 1565 and 1577; *Anonymous Plays*, third series, 1906; *Tudor Facsimile Texts*, 1907.

Marie Magdalene, by Lewis Wager, 1566–67; edited by F. G. Carpenter, 1902; *Tudor Facsimile Texts*, 1908.

Jacob and Esau, 1568 ; *Dodsley*, ii ; *Anonymous Plays*, second series, 1906 ; *Tudor Facsimile Texts*, 1908.

The Three Ladies of London, by R. [obert] W. [ilson], 1584 and 1592 ; *Dodsley*, vi ; *Tudor Facsimile Texts*, 1911.

The Three Lordes and Three Ladies of London, by R. [obert] W. [ilson], 1590 ; *Dodsley*, vi ; *Tudor Facsimile Texts*, 1912.

The Conflict of Conscience, by N. Woodes, 1581 ; *Dodsley*, vi.

The Contention between Liberalitie and Prodigalitie, 1602 ; *Dodsley*, viii.

For the works of the greater Elizabethan dramatists see the standard editions.

CHAPTER VII

W. Hone—*Ancient Mysteries Described*, 1823 ; chiefly valuable for the light it throws on eighteenth-century survivals of the religious drama.

For the S. George plays, see A. Beatty, *The S. George and Mummers' Plays* (reprinted from vol. xv of the Transactions of the Wisconsin Academy of Sciences, Arts, and Letters, 1906). Versions of these plays are in Chambers and Manly ; others, together with evidence for their performance in the last and present centuries, in *Notes and Queries*, third series, x. 466 ; xi. 271 ; xii. 493 ; fourth series, x. 417 ; fifth series, ii. 503 ; x. 489 ; tenth series, v. 155 ; vi. 481 ; vii. 30 ; and in A. Beckett, *The Wonderful Weald*, 1911.

For *The Coronation of Elizabeth*, see Morley, *Memoirs of Bartholomew Fair*, 1859.

For modern Christmas plays in various countries, see C. A. Miles, *Christmas in Ritual and Tradition*, 1912.

INDEX

THE BOOK

This classical on ageless Christian Drama aims to present periods when actually dramatic performances or 'Religious Drama' were used to teach Biblical and Hagiographical subjects to the general public. This short sketch of one of the arts of Christian Church presents Origin, History, and Development on the subject with Illustrations and Bibliography; in chronological order.

Since beginning the significance of some special Christian festivals was shown through these performances. Then came up the Liturgical Drama in the Middle Ages (12th & 13th centuries). During this phase, plays were acted within or near the Church, based on stories from the Bible and of the Saints. The language of the Liturgical Drama was Latin, and the music was also used in the form of incidental dance and processional tunes. Eventually, the plays came under secular sponsorship and began to be presented outside the Church; the local populace became involved across whole of Europe. Plays were then presented by the Christian Communities in the vernaculars, based on stories from the Bible. By the 13th century Miracle Plays, also called as Saints' Plays, came into picture. These plays used to present, a real and fictitious account of the life, miracles, or martyrdom of a Saint. Later, they were banned by Henry VIII in the mid-16th century.

Morality Plays (15th & 16th centuries) were an allegorical drama, wherein characters personify moral qualities (such as charity or vice) or abstractions (such as death or youth) thereby teaching moral lessons. However, Interludes were referred as dramatic scenes presented usually with music and singing in between of a play when a little fun was required for enlivening the audience after a serious scene. The phase of Elizabethan Drama (late 15th & 16th centuries) covered the works of Christopher Marlowe and William Shakespeare. It was during this time frame that permanent theaters were built.

During the early 17th century Catholic Church splitted up and many new Christian organizations called Protestants were formed. As a result a new Protestant religion called Puritans evolved. The Puritans believed that man must follow the Bible exactly and try to communicate directly with God. In order to communicate with God there had to be no distractions from their religion. Puritans rather continued to immerse themselves in their belief by avoiding any such distractions. This resulted in the end of 'Religious Drama' but the Author hinted at its revival during the years rolled by.

This living book of Biblical record covers subjects like Art, History, Poetry, Anthropology, Dramaturgy, Christianity, and Biographical narratives of various Saints; and is meant for Historians, Artists, Litterateurs, Christian Laity, Church Clergies, Students and Researchers.

THE AUTHOR

Mr. Gordon Crosse of New College, Oxford and Lincoln's Inn, authored, co-authored and edited many books including *Shakespearean Playgoing, 1890-1952; A Dictionary of English Church History;* and *Fifty Years of Shakespearean Playgoing.*